How to Collect Rent
and other adventures in property management

J. Elaine Taylor

with David A. Blum

ISBN: 150027366X
ISBN-13: 9781500273668

DEDICATION

To our many, many tenants who paid the rent on time and only called us for legitimate repairs. Thank you so much.

CONTENTS

ACKNOWLEDGMENTS

First and foremost a special thanks to all of our clients who entrusted us with your real estate investments which represented your early retirement and children's college fund. We would also like to thank our friend and attorney in the Central Valley of California who preferred to remain anonymous. You are possibly the only attorney who doesn't try to make a Federal case out of evictions. Another huge thank you goes out to Sharyn Abbott who encouraged us to write books as an income source and marketing tool. Finally, we would like to acknowledge all the tenants both good and bad who gave us fodder for this book.

Introduction

A Landlord's How-to Handbook

Congratulations. You have decided to manage your residential rental properties yourself. Maybe you feel like your property manager just takes ten percent of the rent money and doesn't do much else. Maybe you've driven by your properties and think that your property management company has allowed a bunch of low-life tenants to move in, and they are not only trashing your place but making the whole neighborhood unsafe.

Or maybe you feel your property management firm is gouging you on repairs. They probably are.

On the other hand, you may not realize is how much your property management firm has been shielding from you. They may be taking calls daily from a whining tenant who is never satisfied with the property and threatening to withhold rent until their demands are met. They may be working to avoid an eviction because a good-paying tenant had a costly emergency and is catching up on rent through a payment plan. Collecting rent is definitely not always as easy as it looks, and there are legal issues that your property management firm is very familiar with and you may have never heard about.

Maybe the decision to manage your own rentals has nothing to do with management companies. Perhaps you tend to be "hands on" in everything that you do. You are a do-it-yourselfer, and you are reading this book because it will help prepare you for managing your properties effectively without a lot of unpleasant surprises.

How to Collect Rent and other adventures in property management tells you the ins and outs of managing single-family homes and small multi-units on your own without hiring a property management firm. We, the authors of this book, have managed properties for nearly ten years, having first started as landlords of our own properties.

Although we took classes and seminars and read several books on property management, none of this "education" reflected the practical knowledge we received by actually dealing with tenants. Therefore, a lot of our expertise comes from first hand experience and we have actually made our share of mistakes. However, mistakes became one of our best teachers, and by reading this book you can avoid many problems we struggled with that are associated with managing rental properties.

Eventually we became licensed real estate brokers in order to manage other people's rental properties. In addition, we started an eviction service to help other owners oust their deadbeat tenants. Many these owners were sick of dealing with their rentals and handed their "headaches" over to us. The experience of managing so many properties gave us even more practical knowledge that we can share with you.

When it comes to managing properties and dealing with tenants, there is always a story to tell.

Renting is a cycle. The cycle beings with an empty unit that needs to be made "rent ready." The second part involves finding a tenant, then dealing with tenant issues and collecting rent. Finally the cycle ends with the tenant vacating the property. You can begin reading at whatever point you are at in the cycle. The idea of this book is to make collecting rent the longest and easiest part of the cycle.

We hope you will read the entire book and then use it as a guide for wherever you are at in the rental process. For those of you starting out in the rental business, read the book from beginning to end and pay special attention to Chapter Two through Chapter Eight. Focus on finding a good rental application or creating your own to ensure you obtain the necessary information to sufficiently check out potential tenants.

In addition, find a good rental lease. Enlist the help of an attorney to create a functional lease that will protect you and stand up in court. The lease should reflect your property issues which will vary if you have a house versus a duplex, have property in a city with rent controls, or are leasing a condominium in a large complex. Matters specific to your property may include whether or not you have a swimming pool, if you will allow smoking in your property, if the property is located in the country or in the city.

If you are in the unfortunate position of dealing with a tenant who is not paying rent, start with Chapter Ten and read through Chapter Fourteen. Chapter Thirteen discusses the eviction process. If you are conducting your first eviction you probably should hire a good eviction attorney to help you through the ordeal. Chapter Fourteen contains true stories of a few of our more "unforgettable" evictions.

In this book, we do not discuss being a landlord in areas with rent controls. However, most aspects covered in this book apply wherever you own rental property. San Francisco, for example, not only has rent controls, the city has tenant unions making evictions even for non-payment of rent very difficult.

Wherever you own rental property, be it in San Francisco, California or Jacksonville, Florida, you will need to learn and follow the landlord tenant laws. These laws vary from state to state. You can search online for informational websites to learn more about the laws that apply specifically to the state where you own property. We also recommend that you also consult with an attorney who is knowledgeable with the state and local tenancy laws. *The following serves as a disclosure: We are not attorneys and nothing in this book is purported to be legal advice. We are merely sharing our knowledge and experience of property management with you for informational purposes only. For any questions regarding laws, contracts, leases, tenants rights etc., consult with your attorney.*

If you discover that managing properties is not your thing, don't give up on residential rental properties. In the final chapter, we have included information on how to select and negotiate with a property management firm to find the best company who can take care of your properties while your tenants pay your mortgage and your equity in the property grows and grows.

Chapter One

Managing Your Properties

Managing rental properties may seem easy: find a tenant, sit back and collect rent. Unfortunately, there is quite a bit more to the job than that, and so being a landlord is not for everyone. This book will go into detail about many of the issues you will probably encounter when you manage your own rentals.

If you are goodhearted, kind, full of love for your fellow man, and want to stay that way, we highly recommend you read the true stories in this book and follow the recommendations in the last chapter. Managing rental income properties will harden you and make you a more cynical human being. Guaranteed! It's the name of the game, there's no avoiding it.

Do You Have What It Takes?

Once upon a time after putting in an offer for our first income property, we found out that the current tenants were paying below market rent. In order to make the deal work financially, we would have to come in and immediately raise rents by a least a $100 a month to reach market value. We found this would mean raising rents on three little old ladies with limited incomes. My partner and I discussed the situation and decided to get out of the deal because we didn't want to be "bad guys" and raise rents on people who couldn't afford it. The practical aspect was by raising rents the women would likely move creating three vacancies which would create a potential negative cash flow issue very soon after closing.

Still determined to purchase rental income properties, we eventually purchased a multi-unit with a couple of little old ladies, but in this deal it would not be necessary to raise the rent on them in order to make the finances work. One lady moved before the property even closed and we were able to bring the new tenants in at market rents, but the other lady stayed. She had lived there for about thirty years and the previous owner had never raised her rent. She was paying nearly half of what the other tenants were paying. We decided to raise her rent by ten percent, which was only $35 a month, and still her rent would remain significantly below market. She took the notice in stride, and by the time rent was due the next month, she was dead.

Do you still think you have what it takes?

You Have To Be Tough

In another unit, we had an independent woman in her nineties who was starting to forget things in a detrimental way. She often would start cooking something, forget about it, and let it burn to a crust filling the apartment full of smoke. She was creating a fire hazard. We had no choice but to tell her to move.

People over forty usually make the best tenants in that they tend pay rent on time and often want to stay forever, but they do keep getting older.

Then there's the issue of children. You have to be tough enough to possibly evict families with small children. You have to be able to say, "I'm sorry your baby is in the hospital, but you still have to pay the rent."

A fellow landlord once gave us a line that he uses with his tenants who have kids. His credo is so good and important we have used on some of our own tenants who were lousy rent payers.

He tells parents, *"One of the best things you can do for your children is to pay the rent."*

His philosophy has helped ease some of the compunction we have felt when conducting an eviction on parents with small children has been necessary. Unfortunately, paying rent is a concept many parents don't understand and are completely unaware that giving their child a home creates stability. They don't realize that paying rent sets a good example for their kids to follow and will help them become successful later when they grow up and have children. The tenants have figured out that you -- the land-lord -- don't want to evict, and even if you do, will have to jump through legal hoops to get them out. They know they have time, and they don't care. They are oblivious to the fact that moving all the time to escape creditors and the sheriff pounding on the door has a negative effect on their children.

Many tenants think that when the rent is due, you *owe* them something. They forget, they're living in your house, and you don't owe them anything than what was signed to in the lease. These tenants will come up with a myriad of minor problems with the house – the same kind of problems that you live with in your own home and don't give two thoughts about, like the heater makes a sound when it turns on – and expect you to fix it before they part with the rent money.

Most tenants will be as nice as can be to your face -- you're the landlord after all, but they will be gossiping and badmouthing you behind your back. Count on it!

Some of your tenants will come up with bogus legal in-formation that sounds like it should be true and spout off as if it were fact. They may threaten to sue you if you try to evict them. Other tenants are more savvy and will simply call the local housing authority to try and get them to condemn the house. That action will bring you a demand for repairs from the city, which is more of a nuisance than anything else. But still, tenants will seek revenge simply because you want them to pay the rent on time. If any of this bothers you, read Chapter 17 on finding a good property manager.

Time and Distance

One of the first things you need to decide is if you actually have the time to spend managing your own properties. If you only have one or two houses in town, they shouldn't take up a lot of your time. But if you own several, there will be a significant time factor to consider. The further away the property is from your home or work, the more time it is going to take from your day commuting back and forth. In fact, long distances create other considerations such as gas fill-ups or even overnight stays at a motel and airfare.

One of the biggest time consumers is driving back and forth to show a property. Not all potential tenants can be at the rental based upon your convenience. Many arrived late, and some don't even show up, so you drove out for nothing.

There will be several other occasions throughout the month where you need to go out to the property, possibly to deal with repair issues, post a notice on the door, or just drive by to see how things are looking.

Living next door to your tenants has the proximity advantage, but has the disadvantage that your tenants will be watching you like a hawk. We started out in this business by purchasing a six-plex and lived in one of the units.

The tenants thought we were rich to begin with, and since we worked out of our home and could make our own hours, it seemed to them all we did was sit around and collect rent. We wish! They kept track of when we left, how long we were gone, and when we returned. It was a bit unnerving, but didn't make sense to hire a property management firm, since we were real estate investors – albeit novice -- and lived right next door.

My partner knew a woman who owned a rental located across the street from her own home. In her case, it wasn't so much the tenants were watching her – she was watching them. She couldn't leave them alone, and her tenants couldn't keep the yard up to her standards, or for that matter keep the house clean enough to her liking. She also kept getting involved in their personal business. Needless to say, she couldn't keep long-term tenants and who left her place a mess. She gave up and sold the property.

Buying a rental right next-door or living in a multiplex with your tenants is workable but far from ideal. However, you may already be in that situation, and it is not yet time to sell so it might be time for you to move.

Detach

You need to emotionally disengage from the drama going on in your tenants' lives. Some tenants will tell you convoluted sob stories, which may or may not be true, usually with the hope that you will forgive the late fees or reduce the rent. Tenant problems are not your problems, even if their problems are preventing them from paying the rent.

Your tenants may throw wild parties every weekend, or smoke inside your home, sneak in a pet, or have relationships with people you don't approve. A good lease and adequately checking out your tenants beforehand will help take care of some of these issues. For the most part – as long as they are not doing anything illegal or destroying your property – leave your tenants alone.

You need to be able to detach from what your tenants are doing to your property. Much to your dismay, the tenants may paint the walls dark purple and think it's beautiful, they may neglect to water the roses you planted with care, or they simply may not keep the place as neat and trimmed as you would like. Your tenants may not be intentionally destroying your rental, but they are "hard" on the property. Maybe they let their children run amok and destroy the expensive shades you put in all the windows, or smear their dirty hands on your freshly painted walls. If a tenant's lack of concern about your property drives you crazy, either hire a property management firm or find other lucrative investments for your money.

Although most landlords can manage their own properties with more care than a property management firm, owners also have an emotional and financial investment in the rental that a property management firm does not. If you cannot disengage from your properties, think twice about managing on your own and hire someone to help you.

My partner and I have heard many stories from home-owners crying because the tenant left the place trashed. The tenant didn't purposely damage the place, they just didn't do anything to keep it up. When the owner took possession, the carpets had never been cleaned, the tubs had never been washed, there were fingerprints on the walls and scratches on the floors and countertops. The tenants didn't water and weed the owner's per-fectly manicured lawn and cared less about the roses by the front door, now dead. Tenants who are actually willing to do and pay for upgrades on your property are rare, so don't count on it.

Legal Issues

If you are going to manage your properties yourself, you need to know the laws in your state regarding tenant/landlord issues. Laws vary from state to state. If Colorado does it one way, that doesn't mean the same applies for Kentucky. For instance, some states require twenty-four hour notice before entering a property, some forty-eight hours, and some don't require any notice at all.

After you have learned the landlord tenant laws in your state, you must follow the law to the letter. All it takes is one angry tenant to run to their attorney and you will be getting nasty letters from the attorney threatening to sue, or citations from the county or city. We've had tenants complain to the housing authority be-cause we couldn't get something fixed *only because they refused to let the service provider enter the house*...oh, and they also happened to be a month behind in rent.

Often bookstores will carry books that explain landlord rights and responsibilities as required for a particular state. However, books on tenant's rights explain the law much better and are easier to read. It's good to know what your tenants know so you can be one step ahead of them.

Questions To Ask Before Managing Properties

Answering the following questions will help you determine if you can successfully manage your own properties, and if it is a job you actually *want* to do:

- Is the property close enough that I can accommodate the driving distance from my work and home?

- Do I have time to deal with tenant issues?

- Am I well organized?

- Do I prioritize well?

- Am I flexible in my thinking and can I adjust to alternatives quickly?

- Am I familiar with or can I adequately learn about my state's landlord/tenant act?

- Am I familiar with federal laws regarding housing?

- Am I familiar with state and local laws regarding tenant's rights and landlord responsibilities?

- Will managing properties interfere with my job/family or recreational life?

- Will I be able to handle a tenant emergency 24/7?

- Do I have someone who can handle tenant issues while I am out of town or on vacation?

- Do I like dealing with roofers, contractors and handymen? Or can I make repairs myself?

- Do I have the emotional and mental stamina to deal with the intimate lives of my tenants?

- Do I have the stomach to demand that the rent is paid regardless of the tenant's circumstances?

- Can I deliver bad news without feeling bad about doing so?

- Am I capable of preparing and filing the legal paperwork myself as much as the law allows? (You can always hire an attorney or paralegal for this, but that's more money out of your pocket.)

- Do I understand the eviction process, how long it takes and the costs involved?

- Am I okay with frequent small claims suits against the tenants to recover damages when they leave the property trashed?

- Do I have experience with or can I learn about corporate or personal credit/collections?

If you can answer an enthusiastic *YES!!* to most of the above questions, then property management is the job for you. If not, hire a professional and save yourself a lot of headaches.

Chapter Two

Vacancies

An empty unit can become a major headache. Every month of vacancy is costing you money and creating an insurance risk. Vacant houses are vulnerable to squatters and being vandalized. If your insurance carrier finds out your property has been un-occupied for over 30 days, they may either cancel you or refuse to cover certain claims. If you have a vacant house and someone is already breaking into your property, you may be tempted to take the first tenant who comes along.

Securing your property is preferable than rushing to take a substandard tenant. Ask the neighbors to keep a look out for any kids or vagrants hanging around. Consider installing a security system; the new tenants would also like that. In rough neigh-borhoods, you may need to board up windows and install quality deadbolts on all the doors. Remember to change all the locks after a tenant leaves. You never know how many copies they made and to whom they gave keys.

Determining Rent

One of the first things you need to do when you have a vacancy is to determine what kind of rent you can get for the property. First, take an unbiased look at your property and answer the following questions:

- What kind of cars are parked in the neighbor's driveways and along the street?

- Do most of the people in the area rent or own?

- Are the denizens of the area white collar, blue collar, or barely employed?

- Who lives in the neighborhood? Families? Singles?

- What are other nearby and similar properties renting for?

The type and age of cars people in the neighborhood own will give you a good idea of the prosperity in the area and a clue to the type of people who will want to rent your property. Whether most of the people in the neighborhood rent or own will tell you if the area will continue to be nicely maintained or start to go downhill. The occupation of the denizens will help tell you how much rent you can receive, but also of the expectations your future tenant might have. A busy professional will often expect the place they rent to be newly remodeled and pristine; while blue collar workers are often willing to put in some "sweat equity" in order to bring the rental to the condition they prefer. Neighborhoods with schools and parks nearby will probably attract families with children, whereas more trendy neighborhoods tend to attract more singles or childless couples.

You may think your property should rent for $1000 a month -- after all, that's what it will take for you to just break even -- but if the type of renter who is attracted to that neighborhood can only afford $500, you will have a empty property for a long time. To find out how much something should rent for do a "property rental evaluation."

Begin your evaluation by comparing rents in the same subdivision. Drive the neighborhood and call on every "For Rent" sign you see and find out how much rent your competition is asking. Also inquire about the number of bedrooms, bathrooms, square footage, and any amenities in order to ascertain how the property compares with yours. If the landlord is asking several hundred less in rent than what you want for your property, the landlord may not necessarily be stupid -- the landlord may be realistic.

In many cities, the rent can change from block to block depending on the type of neighborhood. You might find a house rents for $1200 and a similar house just a block away will only command $800. Why? Well, it can be a variety of reasons from a different school district, a change in demographics, or that particular block has a very bad reputation.

Next go to the classifieds and see what similar properties are renting for. Then take it one step further, especially when you're first starting out. Call on the ads as if you are a potential tenant, go see the interior of the property and compare it to yours.

Notice the exterior and the curb appeal of the rentals you are investigating. Perhaps you are looking at a house with the same size and number of bedrooms as yours, but one house has interesting architectural features and the other is just a plain rectangular box. Guess which one can command the higher rent?

The interiors can make a huge difference in how much rent you can receive. One of our vacancies needed fresh paint and new carpet. The living room windows didn't get a lot of light, so instead of painting the walls off-white, we used pure white. We also found a lighter color carpet for about the same price as the "rental grade" tan. The effect was beautiful. With the bright white walls, the place looked clean and huge compared to the other similar rentals we had looked at. Those places had a dingy lived-in look while ours sparkled. We took a risk and asked a hundred more a month than what the competing rentals were asking. We got our price without question and a great tenant who paid on time and took excellent care of the property. You may be able to receive a higher monthly rent just by brightening your place up a bit.

Does your rental have special qualities that will enable you to command a higher rent. Does it have views of mountains, ocean, or city lights? Does it have quick access to the beach, hiking trails or shopping? All of these amenities work in favor of higher rent rates.

Another factor in determining price is rental availability. Several FOR RENT signs in your property's general vicinity indicates a tenant's market and you may end up lowering your asking price. When FOR RENT signs are rare, and the advertised rentals are sparse, you have a landlord's market. Unless your property is priced ridiculously high, you should be able to command the rent you want.

Ultimately the market will tell you what the correct rent amount should be. If you are getting a lot of calls and many of them are willing to take the rental sight unseen, you may have it priced too low. When you have it priced too high, you will receive a lot of "thanks but no thanks." However, if you have a newly built property or one that has been recently remodeled, consider pricing it on the high end of market. Let's say rents for a similar house as yours go for $800 - $900 a month. You might try pushing it a bit and see if you can get $950 or $1000. If there are no takers, you can always lower your asking price.

Advertising

Paying for a classified ad in the local newspaper used to be the preferred method of advertising your rental. A good ad could, and sometimes still does, generate a lot of inquiries about the property. In some areas using the classified ads is the only way to get a vacancy rented. However, advertising through a classified ad usually runs over a hundred dollars a week, and that's expensive, especially if you have to run it for several weeks. When advertising this way, include some of the features of the property: fenced back yard, garage, washer/dryer hookups, new carpet, remodeled, good schools, etc.

Knowing the best time to place a newspaper ad can save you money. Often people who live in low-income areas do no require a lot of time to move. We have had prospective tenants who will put in an application on Friday expecting to move in on Saturday. If you have property in such an area, your prospective tenant will usually read the Wednesday and Sunday paper for rental ads. Also, they tend to want to move the last week of the month, before having to pay next month's rent at the old place. Therefore, the best time to place a classified ad is during the last two weeks of the month.

Because of the expense and the "hit or miss" phone calls, only use newspaper classifieds as a last resort. The problem with newspaper classifieds is the reader cannot tell where the neighborhood is simply by reading the ad. They may want something close to work, or in a specific school district. The house you are renting may have all the qualifications they want, but when they hear it is in a rough neighborhood, they say, "Bye, bye." We've even had people get hoity-toity with us and imply we're terrible people for renting a property in a particular neighborhood they wouldn't live in.

To solve this, we often include the address on the top line of the ad, creating another line and adding to the cost. We know of one person who will put in the address and not the phone number in his classified advertising. The only way people are able to call is if they drive by the property and see the sign. This way, when they call, they have seen the exterior of the property and the surrounding neighborhood and are still interested.

Craigslist.org is a great place to advertise your rental, is completely free, and your ad runs around 45 days. Craigslist.org offers plenty of room for you to put in a lot of details about the property and you can include pictures. We have rented many properties through Craigslist.org and prefer it over the newspaper classifieds.

When advertising over the internet, you need to be aware that some of your responses will be to scam you. Every time we have advertised in Craigslist.org, we have gotten an email from someone who sounds perfect for the place...almost too perfect.

Regardless of how perfect they sound, we have them go through the same routine that is required for all our applicants. This procedure screens them out, the scam artists usually go no further. Remember, potential tenants need information about the property, but not about you, nor do they need any money from you. You need information about anyone who wants to see your property, let them supply it to you. Allow interested callers come see the property and fill out an application, if they can't do that, rent to someone else. Repeat: Do not give callers any personal or financial information about yourself.

If you advertise in any medium where your words are in print, you need to remember: *you are advertising to rent the property, you are not advertising for someone in particular to rent your property*. In other words, you can't even give the slightest perception of discrimination in your ad.

Therefore, only talk about the amenities of the property, and say nothing about who you have in mind to rent the property. Avoid something like, "This place would be great for an older couple." Also don't say anything about the neighborhood that could be construed as bigoted such as mentioning a predominant race that lives in the area. Keep it vague: nice neighborhood, good schools, near shopping. Don't say: upper middle-class white neighborhood, and play it safe and don't even say synagogue, mosque or churches nearby.

We have found the best form of advertising is a nice big

FOR RENT

sign. It is also one of the cheapest. In the past, we used expensive signage with our logo printed on it. Inevitably our beautiful signs were stolen. Now we purchase cheap 12x15 outdoor signs with a flimsy metal holder and stick the sign in the front yard. If these low-priced signs are stolen or blown away, it doesn't cost very much to replace. We also put a large FOR RENT sign on the inside of one of the windows for additional reinforcement.

As property managers, one of the things we do is look at other people's FOR RENT signs. Often, they are very small, and unless you are looking would not even notice them. Sometimes the landlord has a nice big sign but the phone number is written in small, thin numbers that you have to get right up next to the sign in order to call. More times than you might think, the landlord has written in information about the property, but forgot to put in the contact phone number. We use large yard signs and have our phone number in big, black, bold numbers so a prospective tenant can call from their car.

However, if your property is located off the beaten track so that very few cars drive by, a sign in the front yard will not get the property rented. We were managing some properties with exactly that problem. They were nice homes on side streets in a sub-division. Very few people ever drove down those streets. We had our big FOR RENT sign in the window with our phone number clearly visible from the street – which very few people saw. We advertised in two separate newspapers and the people who called on those ads did not want to live in those particular neigh-borhoods. Craigslist didn't work either because the demographics of the neighborhood were residents who were not computer savvy. We tried for months to get those properties rented and none of our advertising was working. The few calls we received turned out to be applicants who could not afford to rent the property.

We finally bought two bright yellow poster boards and some colorful magic markers and constructed two of the following signs:

HOUSE

FOR RENT

ADDRESS

There was no phone number on the sign, and the address was big enough someone could read it from the car. We placed the signs on busy corners entering the subdivision. The phone number was on the FOR RENT sign at the property, so the potential tenants had to find the house in order to call. By making our own homemade signs, we rented the property within a week. Better yet, we had another property that we weren't quite ready to advertise and got that rented too. The tenant looked at the house on the sign and asked if we had anything else a little cheaper, and we told her about the soon-to-be-available property. She was willing to clean it up herself in exchange for some money off the rent.

It's amazing what a sign can do. What's nice about a sign is that only people who are willing to live in that neighborhood will bother calling.

Showing Property

When we are experiencing a tight rental market we will set a time to show the property individually to each person as they call. In a landlord's market when we receive a large response to a property or if the distance is prohibitive, we will arrange an open house usually on a Saturday afternoon. We tell people we will be at the house at 2pm and see who shows up. Sometimes, even though we received nearly a hundred calls, and many of them said they would definitely be there -- no one shows up. This is rare, but it has happened. Usually a small fraction of people who said there would be there actually arrive.

Whenever we promote an open house, we call back the people who inquired about the property the evening before the open house. Most people don't answer, and we leave a concise and clear message as to the address and the time of the open house. Instead of giving a range of time – like the house will be open from 2-4 – we tell them exactly what time the open house will start (say 2 o'clock) and don't say how long it will go. This way, if very few people show up by 2:30, we can leave instead of hanging around an empty house for two hours. Besides, we want the tenant who shows up promptly at 2 o'clock, and not the one who dilly-dallies and shows up at five minutes to four.

Safety Precautions

We have never managed properties in areas where we felt we needed to bring a gun, but we know people who do manage in those types of areas and who do bring guns. Although we manage properties in some fairly rough neighborhoods, we still don't bring a gun. On the other hand, we don't show vacancies alone, we take safety precautions, and we don't go at night. Even in the best neighborhoods, we take certain precautions.

When a tenant comes to a managing office, they will usually take a copy of the driver license before showing the rental. When you are working out of your home and meeting someone at the property, this is not a possibility.

Here are a few safety precautions you should take whenever you go show a property.

- You do not want tenants to know where you live, so never have them meet you at your house, nor give them your home address to mail the rent.

- Before leaving, tell someone where you are going and who you will be seeing.

- Don't look rich, drive the beater car instead of the Mercedes when showing homes.

- Dress for the income of the neighborhood, wear your designer clothes someplace else.

- Park in a well-lit, visible location.

- Never park in the driveway! Someone can park behind you and block your escape.

- Before getting out of your car, look around. Is there any questionable activity in the area?

- Stay in the car until the applicants arrive. Let them get out of their cars first, if there is something about them making you uncomfortable, simply drive away.

- Don't show fear. There are certain types who feed on fear and if they sense you are afraid will be tempted to try something.

- Keep your keys in hand, they can be used as a weapon to scratch an assailant.

- Bring a fully charged cell phone.

- Bring someone with you. They stay in the car or remain outside while you show the rest of the house.

- If you are alone, let the applicants enter the house while you wait outside.

- If someone wants money, keep a twenty or so and give it to them. Don't carry a lot of cash, but a little cash might make them go away.

- Keep doors open while you show a property.

- Choose flight over fight.

Rather than answering the phone, all calls go into voice mail so interested applicants must leave a message if they are serious about seeing the property. In order to receive a call-back from us, they will have had to leave a working and correct phone number. If someone wants to pull some "funny business" they tend not to want make it easy for the cops to trace them.

Another tip is to avoid displaying fear. My partner and I have both have been in iffy situations while showing properties and collecting rent. Once we realized our vulnerability instead of panicking, we remained calm and acted natural.

One time we were conducting an open house in a questionable neighbor -- not extremely high crime, but not the safest. My partner was called away on an errand leaving me alone for about thirty minutes. During that time, two men stopped by to see the place, and the next thing I know we're talking in the kitchen and I realized if they had criminal intent I was completely cornered. Even though the men had done nothing untoward, the realization of my vulnerability set alarms off in my brain. I remembered to never show fear, stayed calm, and as we talked, I casually repositioned myself by the back door. Nothing happened.

Remember most people are basically good and simply want to find a place to live. Nevertheless, taking necessary precautions to ensure your safety is of vital importance. Your life could depend on it.

Chapter Three

Screening Your Tenants

When you are showing a property, sometimes a prospective tenant will say something like, "I have the deposit and first month's rent, when can I move in?" After hearing fifteen other applicants ask if you will work with them on the deposit, it is tempting to take the tenant with the cash and call it a day. Although having a deposit and first month's rent is important, you need to understand that there is about a 50/50 chance that is the only money you will ever see from that tenant. There's also a chance they'll be one of the best tenants you ever had. It's a toss-up.

As a landlord you must learn how to screen your applicants. You need to look beyond a person's nice and respectful demeanor – they want something from you, after all and are putting on their best behavior – but look into their soul in order to determine if they will pay the rent. Since looking into someone's soul is difficult for most people, the next best thing is to learn how to judge people through their behavior and application. You need discernment.

There are state and federal laws against discrimination and this scares many landlords who are unsure how to proceed when it comes to determining who would be a good person to rent their unit. You cannot discriminate against someone for the following reasons: race, color, national origin, religion, sex, familial status or handicap. You can refuse to rent to them for other reasons, the most important being they have previous evictions or can't afford the place. To learn more about discrimination and what you can and cannot do, search the Internet for websites where you can learn more on your own. As always, when in doubt, consult an attorney.

When it comes to renting out your property, be careful. You want someone who will pay the rent on time, who will take care of your property and who doesn't complain a lot. You do not want an eviction. There are plenty of ways to screen tenants for these characteristics and there is no reason to violate anyone's civil rights.

We have developed a screening process for tenants that works with nearly one hundred percent accuracy. When we stick to our method, we find very good tenants that we are happy with and they seem to be happy with us. Our system doesn't fail, but those times when we have deviated from the system -- like before we knew better or when we got desperate -- we ended up with a tenant we wished we hadn't. Whenever we do an eviction, we look back over our own rules to see what went wrong. The rules didn't let us down, we stupidly violated our own standards.

Screening Rules

A huge part of finding a good tenant is to be patient. When you have a vacant house that is taking months to get rented and you are watching your money reserves for future repairs and buying another property going out the door, it can be very tempting to ignore the rules and rent to the first person with cash in hand. Remember -- evictions are more expensive than vacancies. Not only will you have a non-paying tenant, you will have legal fees and additional fix-up costs. Plus, when the tenant is finally gone, you'll have yet another vacancy.

If you follow the five rules in this chapter, it may take you longer to find a good tenant, but you will eventually get a tenant who pays the rent *on time, without being prompted* and stays for many years.

Rule 1: Callers Must Leave a Message

The process of screening tenants starts with the very first phone call. One of the first qualifications you need for a future tenant is for them to be able to leave a message. Paging and/or leaving you a text message does not count. The potential tenant must be able to leave a clear verbal message with a phone number for you to call them back.

The reason your tenants need to be able to leave messages is because you cannot always answer the phone. If they cannot reach you in person, the ability to leave you a message and explain the problem will save you time and aggravation. When you receive the message you can immediately take care of the issue without playing phone-tag that can go on for days. Think of it like this, if your future tenant does not have the ability to leave a message, how totally incompetent is that? The first way to determine if your tenant will leave messages is during the application process.

You can put an outgoing message on your voice mail briefly describing the property you are renting. Include the address, number of bedrooms, bathrooms, square footage, other features, if you will accept pets, rent amount and deposit. A message giving basic information about the property will screen out a lot of people who are simply curious about the property. This type of message can be a big time saver. You won't have to make a lot of return phone calls, only to tell someone how much your property rents for, have them say thank you and hang up.

By listening to the messages left by interested parties, you can tell whether or not to even bother to call back. If you didn't understand the message don't call back. There is already a communication barrier and you haven't even met them. For instance, because we do not speak Spanish, we do not call people back who leave messages in Spanish. Sorry. For the record, we used to return phone calls that were left in Spanish, only to have someone hang up on us when we spoke in English.

Neither do we call people back who speak in such a way we can't understand them regardless of language. This decision came after working with a client who spoke English in a completely incomprehensible way. Some people have accents, but they speak slowly and clearly so you can understand, this woman spoke quickly and mumbled. We kept asking her, "What? Could you repeat that? Come again?" Meetings that should have taken fifteen minutes took hours. Small talk was out of the question.

Transfer language barriers to a tenant who has a repair problem and you are unable to understand what they are trying to tell you. You might think they are talking about a water pipe bursting, when in fact it is a small leak at the faucet. Managing your properties is a business, not a charity service. It takes a lot of time and patience to deal with people who are not understandable.

After your prospective tenant leaves a clear message with a phone number, the next step is to return the phone call. Try to call back promptly, later that same day or within 24 hours. The reason is, they are probably looking at several properties and may forget which property is yours. One exception is if you are only able to show the property on one day during the week -- like Saturday – even if they called on Monday, call them back Friday evening and make arrangements to show the property at the following day. Sad to say, if on Monday you make arrangements to show the property on Saturday afternoon, the likelihood is high that the potential tenant will forget all about the appointment and not show up.

When someone who called about the rental does not answer, leave a message. If they do not have voice mail, cross them off your list.

Rule 2: 10 Minutes

If you do not value your time, who will?

We show a property one of two ways. The first and most preferable is to call the interested party back and set up a mutual time to see the property. The other is to hold an open house at a specific time and day, in which we will tell the callers when we will be at the rental.

Whether we are showing property on an individual basis or an open house, we wait ten minutes for someone to show. If no one arrives in ten minutes, even if we traveled three hours to reach the vacancy, we leave. It is that simple and that easy.

If a prospective tenant calls prior to the appointment time and says that they are running late, we will ask when they will be arriving at the premises. Because they gave us the courtesy of calling, we either wait or reschedule for another day. Remember, practically everyone has a cell phone and they can call and tell you they're lost or stuck in traffic.

The reason we are adamant about applicants showing up promptly is that late is a habit and an indication of a pattern of lateness in other areas of their life. True, just because someone shows up on time doesn't mean they will pay the rent on time. Yet, if punctual people will pay late, it makes us wonder of those who arrive late pay any rent at all?

My partner has suggested that not showing up at the agreed upon time makes the applicant a liar. He doesn't want to deal with liars. Neither should you.

There are several theories about why people are constantly late. One is that that wherever they are, they think they are needed more than where they are supposed to be. Another theory is that they want to control the event and make the grand entrance. Most importantly, they do not respect their time and they certainly do not respect yours. Consider this, if they do not respect your time, it follows that they will not respect you or your property. Besides, if someone does not show up when they agreed, how can you trust them to abide by the rental agreement?

We've spoken to people who have *unsuccessfully* managed their own properties and they admitted waiting over thirty minutes for a prospective tenant to come and be shown the property. The tenant doesn't get to control your time. Late arrivals signal a bad beginning for the tenant landlord relationship, specifically because the tenant has already started taking control. Besides, do you really want to sit around in your car at the rental waiting thirty minutes or more – don't you have better things to be doing with your time?

A few other related points regarding leaving messages and being prompt.

- Being late in many cases speaks to their character or lack thereof.

- The inability to leave a message may indicate they need instant gratification of an immediate answer and cannot wait.

- Safety. As mentioned in the previous chapter, if you pick up the phone and agree to show the house, you have no idea who these people are. They could be setting you up for something unpleasant. If they leave a message and a call back number there is some record of who they are or where they called from.

Rule 3: Potential Tenants Must Fill Out an Application

Common sense tells you that an application is a vital part of the rental process. You need an application so you have a record of the tenants names, phone numbers, and emergency contacts. However, you may be surprised how many would-be tenants try to get in without filling out an application.

When you hear -- "We have the money, when can we move in?" – your response should be to hand them an application. Your thoughts regarding this statement should be whether or not they will have the money for rent again next month and the month after that. A lot of times the reason a tenant "has the money and wants to move in now," is they haven't been paying rent at their current place and are getting evicted. By not paying rent, they've saved up enough money to get into another place.

You might find several instances when you tell prospective tenants -- who have the money and can move in now -- to fill out an application, but they are reluctant to do so. The would-be tenants are probably hiding some unfavorable information about themselves. They can go find another naïve landlord who will let them move in because they have the first month's rent and deposit in cash.

The application will give you some clues to determine if the prospective tenant will pay the rent every single month or not. Some landlords insist that prospective tenants fill out the application while at the property, and if you are new in the business is a good idea for you to follow. In this way, the landlord can query the person more closely and later see if the verbal answers match the application. You can query the would-be tenant about issues important to you not on the contract. For instance:

- How long to you intend to live at the property?
- Why are you moving?
- What is it about this neighborhood you like?
- Tell me more about your kids.
- How did you get along with your previous landlord?

Other questions may help draw out conflicts and drama going on in the applicants' lives that could impact their ability to prioritize and pay rent on time.

When someone is serious about renting, they will be ready to fill out the application at the property. They will have the information with them and be able to fill out the application completely. However, you might want to bring extra pens in case they didn't bring theirs.

Our experience has been if the would-be tenants take an application, we rarely see them again. We don't care too much, but charge a small fee if the prospective tenants want to take the application and bring it back later. The fee is only $10, which pays for some of our gas and the printing costs. You can charge a higher fee that would include credit references if you want, but applicants in the lower priced rental market often don't have that much money to spare, especially if every place they look is requiring such a fee.

After your prospective tenant has filled out the application, look it over to make sure they included all the requested phone numbers and contact information. Sometimes they won't have all the necessary information, but they can fill out what they do have and call you later with what is needed. It is important that they include a working phone number in case you need to call them for any reason.

Your application form should have a space for their driver's license number. You also want to see their driver's license. If the applicants can't show you a driver's license, they may not be who they say they are. Make sure the name on the driver's license matches the name on the application and that the applicant is of legal age to enter into a contract.

You will often be asked how long it takes to check out the application. In theory, it only takes a few minutes to call on the prospective tenant's information. Unfortunately, if you have to leave messages, landlords and employers may take several days to respond, if at all. We tell the applicant we will start calling the next business day but warn them that sometimes it takes a few days to gather all the information. Before you show the property, remind prospective tenants to bring a copy of paycheck stubs or proof of income to help speed up the application process.

Rule 4: Listen and Observe

When prospective tenants come to look at the property, they usually dress and act fairly nice. They take off the "goth" make-up, wear clean clothes, put on a friendly face and are on their best behavior. Alcoholics and drug addicts are able to get it together so they walk in a straight line and appear to be a model citizen. You can't always tell by appearances or pleasant behavior if they will be a good tenant. Therefore, you should listen and observe. Let the prospective tenant do most of the talking.

One thing to notice is their response to the property. We've had people turn their nose up at the property and obviously they don't like it, but for some reason they still want to rent it. Why? Probably because they're desperate. Are they scaling down their expectations and tastes because they have financial hardships and are acting responsibly, or is there some other reason they're willing to rent a place they don't want?

We've actually had tenants insult the house, put in an application and follow-up with us wanting to rent the place. If someone doesn't like your property, this could be a sign of future complainers and tenants who won't stay long. On the other hand, we have rented to people who because of financial hardships were accepting a smaller place until they could get back on their feet. Because of their realistic views of their situation, they were good tenants and paid their rent on time. Unfortunately, they moved when their financial situation improved.

Sometimes prospective tenants seem to like the place, but from the onset have a lot of demands. We've had tenants pull this trick right before signing the lease. All of a sudden they want new blinds, and the carpet isn't as perfect as they would like it. When this happens, it may be a good idea to tear up the lease and go onto the next tenant. They're telegraphing that they are "whiners," and nothing will be good enough for them. You don't want a tenant who has nuisance complaints every month, or refuses to pay the rent until the place is up to their standards.

"Why are you moving?" is an important question to ask all potential tenants. Their answer will say a lot. A good answer is one that makes sense, like the wife is pregnant and they need a bigger place, or they want to live closer to work, family or school.

Questionable answers are:

"My landlord doesn't fix anything." This could be a true statement or it could be a tip-off that they are complainers and the landlord just got fed up. We've noticed that people who are in the process of getting evicted use this one also.

"I'm moving because the owner is selling the house." You need to verify this. A lot of times the so-called owner is a friend or a family member. Also ask yourself why the owner is selling. Usually owners of a property with good, stable tenants want to keep the property.

Potentially bad tenants will telegraph themselves in other ways. For instance, asking for an application without seeing the property is an indication they need to move as soon as possible, i.e. they're getting evicted. Warning: A tenant who wants to move in right away is often a very bad sign.

Beware of any tenant who wants to give you money the minute they see the place and are ready to sign a lease and move in. They're probably being kicked-out someplace else, and the reason they have the money now is because they haven't paid rent for three months to their current landlord. Slow it down, you don't have to hurry into a decision because they are desperate.

Sometimes a prospective tenant will love the place and almost expect that you are going to rent to them. This could be because they know they have impeccable credentials or they are simply trying to get in without you investigating their background. For the record, the applicant with impeccable credentials will be happy for you to check them out.

When an applicant says they are going to call back and doesn't do so, signals unreliability. If they can't follow up with a phone call, will they be able to pay the rent?

Pets

Often applicants will ask about pets. Although several property owners are afraid pets will destroy the property, we like tenants to have pets. Pets seem to have a stabilizing influence on people, and many pet owners will go to greater lengths to feed and house their pet sometimes more so than their kids. However, you should not allow the tenant to have any vicious animals so meet and greet the pets before you allow the tenant to move in. If your insurance company finds out your tenant is housing a vicious animal, they will drop you in a second.

One time we received a letter from our insurance carrier saying they had canceled the insurance on one of our rentals, and the reason given was a vicious animal. This puzzled us because the tenant didn't have any pets. We called the tenant to find out what was going on, and she told me the pit bull next door had gotten into their yard through a break in the fence. She assured me the dog was gone. The insurance company went back and verified this before reinstating the policy.

Pit bull dogs seem to be a current favorite of tenants who are living in rough neighborhoods. When every house is subject to a break-in, who can blame them? If security in the area is an issue, installing an alarm system may be less expensive for the tenant than care and feeding of a large animal. Sometimes we will pay or split the cost of the initial security installation in order to keep a good tenant.

A tenant may admit to owning a vicious animal but promise to get rid of the animal in order to move in. Don't believe it and don't rent to them. No matter what they promised, they'll sneak the animal in, and if a vicious pet gets out and hurts someone you will be sued.

You can call your insurance carrier for a list of animals they will not tolerate.

Before renting to tenants, you should meet everyone who is going to be living in the place including pets. When we were novice landlords, we had a tenant move into a vacant unit who we thought would be perfect. She was single, going to school, working two jobs, and wanted to be a cop. In fact, she had been the cashier when we bought the FOR RENT sign and asked about the place. My partner and I liked her a lot. She wanted to know if we allowed pets. As usual, we told her a small animal would be fine. She said she had a small terrier and it wasn't any trouble. When we heard small and terrier, we assumed Skye or Boston, and let her move in.

After she moved in, a handyman came over to do a few repairs, and he said the dog seemed to be very nice. I didn't think anything about it, until another handyman informed me the dog was a pit bull. A pit bull?! She told me it was a terrier. "A pit bull terrier," he said. She moved rather than give up her dog, but to prevent a similar mishap, make sure you see the pets before you sign the lease.

Children

You must meet the children before committing to rent to tenants. Usually potential tenants will bring their kids along which will save another interview. Observing the kids will give you clues about your potential tenant. Are the kids well behaved or are they acting like spoiled brats? Or do you notice anything odd about the children's behavior?

We had one applicant who brought along her young boy

who was about seven years old. This kid was on some kind of sugar high. His hands were all over the walls and he kept going from room to room. Before the mom had finished filling out the application, he had broken the thermostat and a mini-blind. Although her application indicated she could afford the place, we didn't rent to her. If the applicant's kid are already starting to destroy the place before moving in, think of what your rental will look like when they are gone.

On the flip side, observe if the applicant's child seems too quiet and withdrawn. Every time we have rented to someone with a withdrawn child, we have had to do an eviction. I'm not sure why this is, but our theory is the family is too unstable and the child knows they will not be at one place very long -- there is no reason to make friends, or be friendly.

The Perfect Tenant

Beware of potential tenants who are perfect. We've had a few occasions where the applicants seemed ideal for the house and would make great tenants. They were friendly without overdoing it, and even seemed like people we would enjoy knowing better and socializing with. On the surface their applications looked fine. While talking to them, it would have been tempting to say, "The place is yours."

Regardless of how wonderful any potential tenant seems, do not commit to rent until you have investigated the application!

Fortunately, each time the "perfect" tenant came along, we curbed our enthusiasm. Even though we wanted to rent to them right then and there, we took the application and made only one promise -- that we would get back to them. We were smart, because every single time the "perfect" tenant's application didn't check out. We were looking at a potential problem similar to the movie *Pacific Heights*.

When looking into these "perfect tenant" applications, we discovered even on the surface, things didn't quite didn't fit, and their stories didn't make sense. Digging a little deeper, we found the past tenancies were complete fabrications and employment was unverifiable. We were exasperated because the applicants came off as exactly the kind of people we wanted to rent the house: clean, responsible, employed.

Some people are rental scammers. Their game is to get into a place and stay there as long as possible without paying rent. They eventually get evicted, but in the meantime, they can live someplace up to five months or more without paying any more rent than the first month and deposit which they happily will give you in cash. Part of their game is to lull you into liking them, so you won't check out their application. The next part of their game is to keep promising to get the rent paid while being your best pal, giving them more time. This leads to the final rule.

Rule 5: Always, Always Check Out the Applicant

When you have someone who seems good and nice and you want to rent to them right away, put some reins on it, and check them out. Verifying the application is probably the most important thing you can do as a landlord. You can tell a lot about your prospective tenant by making a few phone calls, and doing some online research. The next chapter details step by step how to check out an application.

Chapter Four

The Application

Many property managers will run a criminal and credit check before renting out a property. The prospective tenant should pay for these reports, but renters in low income areas often cannot afford these fees. We have found other effective ways of checking out a tenant that we used in lieu of expensive background checks.

Good credit doesn't necessarily mean your tenant will pay the rent on time. Unpaid rent will not show up on a credit report unless there are prior judgments or if the previous landlord sent the deficit to collections. Many landlords don't bother with obtaining judgments because of the legal fees and know they still can't get their money. In addition, it seems most landlords are unaware of how to find and use a collection agency. Collection agencies take from thirty to forty percent of what they collect and rarely collect anything. In that respect, when it comes to rental verification, credit reports have limited value.

The good thing about a credit check is you can verify if the social security number the applicant gave you is legitimate, which does come in handy if you decide to send your tenant's unpaid rent and damages to collections.

We have rented to people who told us straight out they had bad credit, but they paid their rent every month on time. You see, if someone has good credit rating that could mean they have credit card debt, or they have a car payment and make paying those bills a priority. Rent, on the other hand, for these people with good credit, may or may not be a priority. If your tenants are ever in a financial bind, which becomes more important – paying the rent on time, or keeping their good credit rating?

Maybe you don't want to rent to an ex-con, but the one we rented to never gave us any trouble. We didn't do a criminal background check and only later found out had been in prison for armed robbery. He was a nice person, had a good job, and always paid the rent on time. If we had known about his criminal history up front, we may not have rented to him, but he turned out to be one of our better tenants.

Don't misunderstand. We're not saying not to perform a credit or criminal background check. If you feel more secure completing these checks, by all means, do whatever is necessary to make yourself feel confident about renting to an applicant. However, background checks are costly and if the applicant is willing to pay application fee then collect that money.

Before spending the fees on the credit check, follow our instructions below. If the application doesn't pass muster, then you can simply pocket the fee and only spend it for those applicants who you seriously want to consider as tenants.

By the way, we do not charge an application fee because we don't run those checks. But we do charge a $10 fee for anyone who wants to take an application with them and fill it out later. If they fill out the application at the property, we do not charge. The reason is, when they take the application with them, they rarely return it. By charging a small fee, it helps recoup our printing costs and gasoline for driving back and forth, and indicates the applicant is serious about renting the property.

We recommend to never rent to someone based solely upon a credit and criminal background check. We think these reports only give a false sense of security and are not true indications of whether or not the tenant will pay the rent since there is no mechanism to report such activities.

Landlords seem to be reluctant or fear calling up a current or past landlord to ask questions. We know this because when our bad tenants have moved on we rarely received a call from their next landlord, although it is possible the bad tenants lied on their application. However, we have rarely received calls from landlords checking on our previous good tenants either. In order to ensure that you rent to a good tenant, you need to verify the application and make sure what the applicant told you is true and that means making some phone calls.

Application Info

A good rental application will help you in the investigation process. You can purchase rental applications at most office supply stores, download one from the Internet, or create your own. If you create your own, you can add questions that are important to you regarding new tenants such as if they smoke. However, consult with an attorney to ensure nothing on the application you create is illegal or violates federal and state discrimination laws.

Your application must contain a statement where the prospective tenant allows you to substantiate any of the information disclosed on the form and will authorize you to perform a credit and criminal background check. The prospective tenant also needs to sign the application. The link below will direct you to a copy of[1] the sample application we use.

Personal Information

Naturally you need the applicant's name and phone number. Also request their social security number, which you will need if you perform a credit check. Legally they do not have to give it to you. A social security number is not necessary to investigate your future tenant, however it is helpful if you decide to send unpaid rent from a previous tenant to collections.

https://docs.google.com/file/d/0B1MGWHPenZQgS1pCRS02aFlSVDg/edit?pli=1

Two important pieces of data you need to collect are the applicant's date of birth and their driver's license. Ask to see their driver's license and make sure the picture looks like the applicant, and that the name on the application is the same as the name on the driver's license. Verify the applicants age to ensure the they are old enough to enter into a rental contract according to the laws of your state.

If the applicant claims not to have a driver's license but drove anyway, take this as a red flag. When someone is driving illegally, you should wonder what else that person might be doing that is illegal and what other matters the applicant may be lying about. If the applicant is underage, the name does not match, or they are driving without a valid driver's license, you do not need to investigate the application any further -- keep looking for a better tenant.

On your application you might want to include some yes or no question that are of importance to you. Some of these questions might be:

- Have you ever been served an eviction notice?
- Have you ever refused to pay rent for any reason?
- Have you ever been convicted of a felony or misdemeanor?
- Does anyone in your household use illegal drugs?
- Does anyone in your household smoke?

If the answer is yes to any of these questions, and the applicant admits so much, you can discuss the issues with them because at least they have been honest with you. When the applicant checks no, investigating and confirming the veracity is difficult. However, if you later find out the information was false, you can use the perjury to invalidate the lease if you so desire.

Employment and Income

The application will have a section regarding employment. You need to know where the applicant works, the name of the company, the address, the type of business, position held, income amount, name and telephone number of the supervisor. Also find out how long the applicant has been at that company. If the applicant has been at the job for less than two years, ask for the same information regarding their former employment. Red flags should go up if the applicant worked at the previous job less than two years also -- it speaks to instability and you will be taking a chance if you rent to them.

You need to verify income. Because of privacy concerns, many companies will not give out income information over the phone. They will require a scanned-in sheet with a signature from the applicant saying it is okay to release the information. When you submit this, it usually takes several days for the employer to get back to you if they respond at all. To speed up the process, ask prospective tenants to bring two recent paycheck stubs. Those applicants on government assistance such as SSI, will be able to provide you with the most recent copy of their award letter.

Even though you have paycheck stubs for income verification, you still need to call the employer. Who knows, your applicant may have been fired yesterday. Call the employer to make certain the applicant still works there.

When you call, you want to ensure that the phone is answered like a legitimate business. Applicants who are looking for a place and don't have a job have their friends answer the phone as if they are the boss. Answering the phone with a "hello" rather than stating the name of the company is a bad sign. If you have questions about the legitimacy of the business, you can see if there is a website and take a drive by the physical location. To ensure a questionable business that you never heard of is not some fly-by-night operation, you can find out how long the company has been in operation. If your doubts about the business have not been satisfied, dismiss the application.

Although employers tend not to disclose income in-formation, they are often happy to provide you with the following information:

- Dates of Employment
- Hours worked weekly
- Position at the company

Be sure this information mirrors what the applicant wrote. Give a few months leeway on employment dates as people remember being hired in the spring, but not the exact date. If your applicant has been on the job for less than two years, also call the previous employer. You do not care about their previous income only how long they were at the job. If your applicant was there less than a year, look for another tenant. When someone cannot keep a job for more than two years, there is a problem.

In cases where prospective tenants cannot or will not provide pay stubs, go on to the next applicant. People who claim to be employed but cannot produce paystubs are probably hiding something -- like the fact that they don't really have a job, or their income comes from illegal sources.

Beware of applicants who claim they are self-employed and work at home. It's possible the "self-employed" applicant is doing a lot of work under-the-table and won't be able to give you any proof of income. The tenant may be dealing drugs or some other illegitimate activity. Applicants who are legitimately self-employed will be able to show you their federal tax return schedule C and E. They should also have a year-to-date profit and loss statement. If a self-employed applicant needs to be licensed, such as a real estate agent, you can go on-line to the state's regulatory agency and confirm they hold the required credentials.

We had one applicant who was self-employed and the name of her business sounded very impressive for someone doing computer work out of her home. We checked a little further into the business, and there really was a business by that name, but with a different phone number than she gave on the application. We called the number of the actual business. Unfortunately, she was not the owner, she was a former employee who had been terminated. Hmm.

One time we had an applicant who was self-employed and we asked for tax returns. He said he was in the process of moving, and his papers were still packed, but he could get us a letter from his CPA, which he did. Unfortunately, there was something kind of hokey about that letter. We couldn't figure out exactly what it was, but our instincts said this wasn't right. Silly us -- still new in the business -- we didn't follow our instincts and went ahead and rented to him. Guess what, from day one after the signing of the lease, we had problems collecting rent. Problems collecting rent always mean an eventual eviction, and he was evicted in less than a year.

Yeah, But Can They Afford the Place?

Many people cannot figure out if they are able to afford the rent or not...sad but true. They may want a four bedroom house, so their children do not have to share a room, and they may want a big fenced backyard for their two dogs, but the reality is their income only affords them a smaller place. They are thinking about their desires, and not the reality of their budget. Therefore, it is up to you to discern if your applicant can afford the rent.

By using a simple calculation, you can determine how much rent the applicant can afford to pay.

If the applicant has no other dependants and has little or no stated credit debt, multiply thirty-three percent of gross monthly income to see if the applicant will qualify. Here is an example:

Rent: $750.00

Monthly Gross Income Verified: $2500.00

$2500.00 x 33% = $825.00.

Based on this calculation, the applicant should be able to afford the unit because $750 is less than $825.

When the applicant has dependents and some debt like a car payment, use twenty-eight percent as the calculation. For example:

Rent: $750.00

Verified Monthly Income: $2500.00

$2500.00 x 28% = $700.00.

Based on this calculation, the applicant does not make enough money to qualify for $750 rent.

If applicant is paying child support, high credit card debt, and a large car payment you can use twenty-five percent for your calculation. For example:

Rent: $750.00

Verified Monthly Income: $2500.00

$$2500.00 \times 25\% = \$625$$

In this case, the applicant cannot afford $750 rent.

When performing these calculations, do NOT include over-time. Overtime can change, from a lot during certain seasons to none during others. Regardless of what the tenant tells you, overtime is not guaranteed. Only consider forty standard work hours at the regular pay rate.

Repeat: Overtime does not count as income!

We made the overtime mistake once, and never again. We rented to the nicest lady, and based on her forty-hour a week wage, she couldn't afford the house; but with the overtime she could more than afford the place. She was older and single. Our experience has been that older, single women make very good tenants, so we rented to her. A few months after moving in, her employer hired a more people and her overtime stopped. She struggled to pay the rent until she admitted she needed a cheaper place. Overtime is not guaranteed, so don't count it, even though your tenant does.

Rental History

On your application ask for the current and previous tenancy information. You need to obtain the applicant's current address, rent amount, how long they lived there, why they are leaving, and the current landlord's name and phone number. Also, equally important, acquire the same information regarding the applicant's previous landlord.

Always verify rental history!

One of the first things you need to look at is the length of residency. You want to find tenants who stay a long time and don't move often because you want your tenants to stay with you several years. Vacancies cost you money. As with employment, length of residency speaks to stability.

Ideally, you will personally speak with both the current landlord and a previous landlord. However, in finding out about the previous tenancy is more important than what the current landlord has to say. In fact, the applicants may ask that you not call their current landlord because they have not told the landlord they are moving. You should respect that request. Please note, you absolutely must check into an applicant's past tenancy. Extremely important! Here's where a lot of red flags pop up.

One of the problems with talking to the current landlord is they may want the tenant out and will tell you wonderful things about the applicant just to get rid of them. The previous landlord has no such qualms and will tend to speak more frankly.

If the applicant is being evicted or has evictions in the past, they're not going to want you to know about that part of their lives, and a previous landlord will tend to be forthcoming about in-formation the applicant prefers you not to know. Therefore, it is very common for prospective tenants to lie on the application. Some tricks applicants pull to hide their sordid rental history is to put down that they owned a house, it was paid for and there is no mortgage information. Or they may claim to have were living with friends, family, husband, and have no previous rental history. Sometimes they will put down the name of a friend who has been prepped to pose as the landlord when you call.

How To Check on the Tenancy

Prior to contacting the either current or previous landlord, you can check the address with the county recorder's office and determine if it is a legitimate residential address. This is public information can be usually found online; but in some areas you may have to make a phone call or go in person to access the data. When in doubt, drive by the applicant's address and see for yourself what is there.

You will be amazed how many "former addresses" turn out to be non-existent. We had one applicant whose "previous address" was actually a medical building. She stated she lived there with her parents. Needless to say, if it turns out the current or former home address was bogus, you need to pass on the applicant and keep looking.

After you have established the applicant has given you a legitimate residential address, check the public records to see if owner's name agrees with who the applicant claims was the landlord. If the owner's name is different than what is on the application, the phone number may be a legitimate property management company or that of a friend posing as the landlord. A property management company will tend to answer the telephone in a professional manner or have a business message on the answering machine.

Let's assume that you've checked on the property address and it is a residential home and the owner's name also matched the name they gave as the landlord. Before calling the landlord, you can take your investigation one step further and verify that the phone number the applicant gave is registered in the landlord's name. A lot of times you can "Google" the phone number or use a reverse directory to confirm that it belongs to the previous landlord. This trick is not 100% foolproof. For instance, if the landlord has an unlisted telephone, the number will not show up. What you might find are indications the phone number on the application has been used when advertising rental properties – a good sign.

We once had a couple applying to rent a house we managed. They gave us a legitimate residential address claiming that was where they currently lived. However, when we searched for the landlord's name in the public records it was not the same name that the would-be tenants wrote on the application. After further scrutiny, we found the person listed on the application owned no property in the county. When we checked the "landlord's" phone number -- it turned out to be a relative of the applicant.

Once you have confirmed that the landlord is a real person

and does indeed own the property, it is time to make contact. Just because the applicant gave you a real property address with the name of the real owner doesn't mean the phone number actually *belongs* to the landlord. You still have to call and confirm. If you call and receive voice mail, rather than leaving a message – they rarely return calls anyway – a better strategy is to call back later.

If a live person answers, ask to speak to the name written on the application. Sometimes the person will tell us we have a wrong number, even though we dialed exactly what was on the application, meaning either the applicant wrote the number down incorrectly or is pulling a fast-one.

When you have the person who claims to be the landlord on the line, rather than revealing that you want former tenancy information, find out how they know the applicant.

Ask: *Joe Applicant used your name as a reference, how do you know him?*

If the person you are calling is a "plant," you can usually catch them off-guard since they won't be sure if they're supposed to be an employer or a landlord or just a reference. The answer may surprise you.

When you have confirmed that you are speaking to the owner or the property management firm, here are a list of questions to ask:

- Why are your tenants moving? See if it matches what they told you.

- Current rent amount? Make sure it is the same on the application.

- How long have your tenants lived at your rental? Confirm that these times are also the same on the application.

- What day was the rent due? This is an important question since the applicant could be paying on-time if they have until the fifteenth of the month and you want your rent by the third.

- Has tenant ever been late in paying rent? If so, how many times in the last twelve months?

- Did the tenant pay your late fees?

- Did or will the tenant receive their full deposit back? This will tell you how they kept the place and if they paid their rent during the last month of their tenancy.

- Did you ever have to start an eviction proceeding against your tenant?

- How many times during the past year did you have to address a repair or complaint issue? You want tenants to call when something is wrong but not three or four times a month.

- Did the tenants give you notice? If the answer is no, you probably will not receive notice when the tenants are ready to move.

- Would you rent to your tenant again?

The final question is critical!

If you can only ask one question, find out if the landlord would rent to them again. A simple yes or no. If landlord says no, we try and find out why, but they may be reluctant to explain. The landlord's reluctance also tells a lot. Many times the landlord won't go into details fearing the tenant could file a lawsuit against them. Regardless of the reason for the "no" response, if someone who has had a relationship with the applicant would not rent to them again, why should you?

Always believe the landlord when they say they wouldn't rent to a tenant again. Always!

One time we called a former landlord and asked the above questions. The tenants paid their rent on time, they took care of the place, but the landlord wouldn't rent to them again, but refused to give a reason possibly fearing a lawsuit. When we spoke to the applicants, the husband shrugged off the landlord's response and blamed it on a personality clash between himself and the landlord.

The couple seemed like a nice family, the previous landlord admitted they paid their rent, so what could go wrong? Ah, everything.

It turned out the husband was a hothead who didn't want to abide by the terms of the lease which he signed. When trying to enforce the lease he became belligerent. He started calling in the middle of the night leaving scary threats on our voice mail. Fortunately, the tenant didn't know where we lived. From that time on, we never rented to anyone that the current and/or former landlord would not rent to again.

We had a tenant who came with good recommendations from her landlord, but after moving in she found every excuse in the book to not pay the rent. She complained about any little thing that was wrong with the property and seemed to be totally helpless. She couldn't even change a light bulb. She was a doctor and could more than afford the place, and could have rented a much larger home, but living alone a three bedroom two-bath house in a gated community was large enough. Nevertheless, she acted like a prima-donna.

We constantly had to communicate with her every month regarding some problem or another. Nothing was ever up to her standards, even though the house was brand new and had never been lived in. Almost every month she paid her rent late and wanted to some money deducted off the rent for reasons that turned out to be stories she made up. Besides trying to weasel out of paying the rent, she begrudgingly followed the lease. We had to cite her several times for not taking care of the yard, which she was required by the lease to do. When she moved, we threw a little celebration party.

We received a request for rental verification from her new landlord. They didn't ask all the questions mentioned above, but did ask the most important one: Would you rent to her again? We replied no. They didn't question us further and we later found out they went ahead and rented to her. She's their problem now.

Other Occupants

Your application should have a section where the potential tenant lists all the names, ages, and relationships of other people who will be living at the property but who won't be on the lease. You can count the number of people who will be living at the property and determine if your place is large enough to accommodate everyone listed. Check the occupancy laws in your state, many states have a minimum number of allowed occupancy based on the number of bedrooms. A rule of thumb might be two people per bedroom, but keep in mind some states do not allow children of the same gender over a certain age to share bedrooms.

Suppose you have a two bedroom house in a state that does not allow children of mixed genders to share a bedroom. A family of four wants to rent the place. Before renting to them, meet the children and determine if the gender combination will work for the home. If the couple has a boy and girl, in theory the girl could sleep in the mother's room and the boy with the father, but in reality that is not going to happen. Also notice if any female applicants are pregnant. Often young couples don't seem to understand that a baby coming along means yet another person.

In spite of who is listed on the application, don't be surprised if during the tenancy people move in and out. Once you have a signed lease, how strictly you want to enforce the number of occupants on the property is up to you. However, your primary consideration is the number of people on the application and how the bedroom situation will work.

We managed a small duplex, and by small duplex, I mean small. One unit was about 300 square feet, with a bathroom so small you had to squeeze past the sink to get to the toilet. The other unit, a bit larger, had an addition about the size of a walk-in closet which counted as a second bedroom. These units were ideal for one person.

We rented the one-bedroom to a very nice, but extremely obese woman. This was the unit where a normal sized person had to squeeze through to use the toilet. She took the place and after a few months brought in her daughter, also extremely large, to live with her. I don't know how they found the space. But they managed and never complained about the lack of space. They lived in the unit for over ten years paying their rent on time.

In the other part of the duplex unit, a single man rented the so-called two-bedroom unit. He brought in his daughter and her small baby. Under the two person per bedroom rule, the living situation was acceptable. Eventually the daughter's boyfriend moved into the place, so there were four people in a place barely over 300 square feet. Technically, the two people per bedroom rule of thumb still held on both units. They paid the rent and didn't complain.

Pet Issues

Whether or not you want to accept pets is up to you. We have found allowing pets makes the place easier to rent. On your application have a place for your potential tenant to list all pets. You want to know if they have cats, dogs, snakes, birds, fish, or any other type animal.

The most common issue with pets is dogs. With a dog, you need to know the breed. Tenants know that they will be unable to bring their pit bull or other uninsurable breed onto the property. They have many tricks to get their vicious animal accepted by you the landlord. Most commonly, they will re-name the breed and call it things like a small, terrier mix. The applicant will tell you how gentle and well-trained the dog is. In order to protect yourself, meet all pets, especially dogs, that the tenant plans to bring onto your property.

If you don't know enough about dogs to decide if it could be an insurance risk, take a picture and let your insurance company decide in writing whether or not the dog will be acceptable. When you meet the dog, also determine if the dog seems friendly toward you or not. We recommend that if the dog doesn't like you, regardless of the breed, to find a different tenant. The last thing you need is a nippy little mutt dog that growls and tries to attack you when you come over to the property.

Beware, applicants often claim not to have pets knowing the landlord will have issues with certain animals. After moving in, the tenant will sneak the pet onto the property. Tenants also have tendency to collect more animals once they are living on the property.

If you find out the tenant has more pets than they claimed, you have a few options: ignore it, make them move, insist they get rid of the animal. The problem with making tenants remove the animal is they will claim to have done so then sneak the pet back onto the property. As long as the pet does not cause insurance issues, the option we prefer is to make the tenant pay an additional pet deposit.

Credit

If you intend to run a credit check on your applicant, you only need their name, social security number, and their signature authorizing you to do so. We ask for banking information solely to help future collection agencies to obtain the money that is owed us. Consider it a bad sign if your applicant does not have a checking or savings account.

Ask about the applicant's car. Besides obtaining the make, model, year, and license plate number, find out how much is owed on the car, as you will consider this in your calculation to determine if they can afford the place. Keep in mind that an older vehicle may break down, and a tenant may have to make car repairs a priority in order to keep their job.

Find out if the applicant pays in child support or alimony, and if so how much.

Consider the size of the applicant's credit card debt and the size of their monthly payments. You don't really care if they owe Sears $100, and Master Card $300. You care about how much the applicant is paying out each month on bills. These amounts need to be considered in your rent affordability calculation.

Emergency Contacts

You won't need to verify the emergency contact information unless you want to. We have never have to call an emergency contact regarding a tenant situation. However, these names and phone numbers can be given to a collection agency if the need arises. And, of course, you may encounter some type of emergency where these people will need to be contacted such as you find the tenant incapacitated in your property.

By carefully checking out the application, you will see for yourself that it becomes easier to find tenants who will pay their rent on-time and take good care of the place. Your evictions will be greatly reduced and your tenants will leave you not because of evictions but because they bought a home of their own or found a larger place for their family. When you are asked by the new landlord if you would rent to them again, you can proudly say, "YES!"

Chapter Five
Refined Screening

When we were new to the business and wanting to learn more, whenever we had a chance we asked for advice from more experienced property managers. One landlord in particular was willing to answer all our questions. We wanted to know about applicants and how she ultimately decided to whom she would rent. She told us she made them fill out an application while there at the property. She would never let them take the application away and come back later. While the would-be tenant filled out the form, she stood around and talked and asked questions. She listened carefully to how they answered and in the end simply used her intuition as to whether or not she would rent to them. She never verified an application.

Wow! We were impressed, but we were also concerned that our own intuition was not that refined.

Nevertheless, if your instincts tell you there's something wrong...there is.

Ultimately when you decide on a tenant, regardless of the application, your intuition should come into play as to whether or not they will be a good tenant. Intuition is not about how someone is dressed or how nice of a car they drive, intuition picks up more subtle clues. So, take a cue from the woman who used solely her instincts, ask questions, observe, and listen.

If something feels wrong about an applicant, yet there is not logical reason for the feeling – trust your gut, and find another tenant.

Neighborhoods

You need to determine if the applicant and the neighborhood are a match. If your goal is to have long term tenants, you can sense if somehow the apartment or house won't work for them, or that they really are misfits for the neighborhood. If you rent to them, they won't stay long.

This is NOT about race, religion or any form of discrimination: it is about whether or not the individual will fit economically and socially in the neighborhood.

For instance, we had a small house we were renting located in a rough neighborhood. At about the same time, two applications came in that would work. One was a family with a small child, the other was a young, single working girl. The mother was a stay-at-home mom, and her husband was a mechanic. The family fit perfectly in the neighborhood, in fact the mother had relatives down the street.

Although the young, single working girl made enough money to afford the place on her own, we saw she didn't fit in the neighborhood. The neighborhood residents worked at low-income, service jobs or were on welfare. The young lady's job was middle-income management. She was simply looking for cheap housing so she could save enough money to purchase a house. We realized, she would be putting herself at risk living in that neighborhood. This young lady, intent on a career with her new car and nice clothes would stick out like a sore thumb and become a potential target for crime. We knew the other tenants would be a better choice for that particular rental.

You should also be considerate of the neighbors and avoid bringing disruptive elements into quiet neighborhoods. One time we had a rental in a nice little neighborhood and a guy came and applied for the house. He drove up blasting music in his car. The neighbor came out and sighed, "I sure do hope you rent to somebody quiet." We took the hint.

Borderline Applicants

When you follow the application guidelines in the previous chapters, you eliminate a lot of potentially bad tenants very quickly. What often happens is you received twenty applications and none of them are very good. The property has been vacant for three months and it's costing you money. You need to get the place rented. Then along comes this application that is borderline. What do you do?

As long as the prospective tenants told you the truth, you may want to consider them. Actually, some of our *borderline* tenants have turned out to be quiet good.

There are basically three areas where someone is borderline:

- Their income just barely qualifies to afford the place
- They don't have past tenant history
- You are unable to confirm some of their information

When you are unable to confirm information, ask the prospective tenant to supply a different kind of proof. Employers often will not return phone calls or be allowed to give out personal data. Unfortunately, the applicant cannot force their employer to give out requested information promptly. Try calling and speaking to the applicant's immediate supervisor.

Landlords who do not call back on rental verification, may be afraid to say anything bad about a tenant. If you left a message that you want information about a tenant, and they don't call back, it could be their way of saying the tenant is no good and they don't want to discuss the situation for fear of reprisal. However, sometimes the landlord just didn't get the message or simply doesn't care if the tenant gets into another place or not. There are a slew of crappy landlords out there, who won't lift a finger for a tenant even to give a truthful verification.

Although it is always best to try and contact the previous landlord because a current landlord may say wonderful things about a tenant just to get rid of them, many tenants don't have a previous landlord.

If your instincts are saying the tenant would be fine, but you're still unsure, increase the deposit amount so the tenant has more to lose by screwing up. Usually landlords charge a month's rent as the deposit and some states will only allow that much. California will allow two month's rent as a deposit, while Alabama will only allow one month's rent as a deposit. However, Alabama has a risk liability fee that you can charge. Since this is a fee, you do not have to refund it.

Another borderline indication is a tenant still living at home with their parents. This could be their first place they are trying to rent. If they are twenty-three and still at home, this is reasonable, but thirty-three and still at home may indicate a problem. It is possible they were forced back home for other reasons besides an eviction such as legitimate economic or health issues. When adults are still living at home, find out the story. Feel free to call the family and make sure the stories match.

If an applicant has no previous rental history, you might get someone in the family who either has a job and/or owns a home to become a guarantor, aka co-signer, on the lease. As a guarantor they are guaranteeing the rent will be paid. This means you can go directly to them and ask for the rent if the tenants don't pay. You may still have to evict, but you can later attach a lien against the guarantor's home or garnish their pay.

Another common issue is that the prospective tenant is borderline financially. When it comes to a tenant who is financially on the edge, we like to hear the words, "You don't have to worry about me, I pay the rent." Note: they need to say this spontaneously and without any prompting or coaching from you.

If you ask whether or not they pay they rent on time, of course, the applicant will tell you exactly what you want to hear. It seems like all applicants would tell their future landlord they pay the rent, but oddly enough, they don't. The tenants who have told us, "you don't have to worry about us, we pay the rent on time," have been excellent tenants. However, they also had a rental history we could verify – probably because they paid their rent.

One time the sister of a prospective tenant put in an application for her brother. He was living out of state and was moving back to be closer to family. She said he was a great guy, but when we looked at his application, he could not afford the rent. The rent would take up over half his income and he had a wife and three kids. What's more, when he arrived, he wouldn't even have a job. He could not afford the rent. That simple.

Still, we continued to check them out. We called their current landlord because they didn't have a previous one. The property manager spoke fondly of the family and verified they were very good at paying the rent. I told her how little he made and how much the rent was, and after paying the rent, they had would have very little left for all the other expenses like food. The property manager said she knew they were in a financially tight situation, but they *always* paid their rent on time. She knew for a fact their kids often had to go without Christmas because they always put the rent first.

Based on that recommendation, we rented to them. What makes this story so amazing, we rented to them based on his sister seeing the place and an application faxed to us. We even did the lease over the internet before meeting the tenants in person. When we met him, he was covered head to toe with tattoos, a look we wouldn't ordinarily put on our A-list. Nonetheless, he became one of our best tenants. We never had to worry about the rent and he was never late. Yet on paper, he could not afford the place. A combination of recommendations and instincts.

Weekly Rentals

Some landlords swear by renting out low income houses by the week. How this works is you find a tenant who can afford the place, doesn't have enough money saved up for a deposit and can't afford to put on the utilities. This often happens when the would-be tenant has been living in a motel. They have gotten used to paying weekly, and the motel is so expensive it is taking away their ability to save up enough to move.

These landlords collect the deposit, but can allow the tenants pay to rent by the week indefinitely or until they can start paying the full rent at the beginning of the month. For the added risk and expense of collecting by the week, the landlord will charge a higher weekly fee. For instance, if the rent was to be $650 a month and the tenant is paid weekly netting between $350 and $400 a week, the landlord collects $175 a week for a total of $700 a month.

Weekly rent is really the least desirable way to manage your properties, although several landlords tout great success using this method. If you want to rent by the week, you will definitely have to supply a stove a refrigerator and may need the furnish the rest of the place as well. For the record, we tried weekly renting with one tenant without success and never tried it again. Find out why someone is living in a motel. It is often – but not always -- because they have been evicted and family/friends refused to take them in.

Social Security and SSI

People with disabilities often qualify for SSI. This is income from the federal government and can have a stabilizing influence on a tenant's finances. Sometimes the tenant will be on permanent disability and sometimes it is temporary.

When an applicant is receiving SSI, find out what the reason is and how long they will be receiving it. If you don't see anything physically wrong with the would-be tenant, the person may be mentally ill, even if you are told otherwise. Be very suspicious. Our experience with people on SSI who are mentally ill is that they seem cogent and can put it together long enough to fill out an application; but they are often unable to consistently pay the rent.

If you suspect mental problems, either have them get someone to guarantee the lease or insist they use a payee. A payee is a responsible person or organization who will handle the tenant's financial commitments. We gladly work with most payees because they put the rent first. If the payee is a relative or friend, you can put them on the lease along with the tenant. That way, if the payee shirks their rent paying duties, the payee will be liable for the unpaid rent. We prefer working with payees who are a part of a non-profit service organization or a religious institution rather than friends or family. A payee is a workable solution if the tenant agrees. Many times the questionable applicant will not want a payee, and if that is the case, you should *not* take a chance on them. Rent to someone else.

With any tenant who is borderline, do one more thing. Make them show you how badly they want the rental. Don't call them and tell them your extra demands – such as an increased deposit, guarantor or payee -- let them call you to follow-up on the application. At that time, you can tell them the issues you have and what they need to do in order for you to rent to them. If they don't call back, they're not willing to put in the extra effort and you don't need them as a tenant.

Don't let a tenant manipulate you into giving them a place. One way they try this is through their desperation, making you feel guilty for not caring about their plight and preying on your kindness. Another way they manipulate is by begging or even crying – which is another good reason to not answer the phone and let them leave messages. If you are a softie and they start any manipulation trick, do not give in. A lot of times, the applicants will not accept no for an answer. If necessary, just hang up and don't mess with them anymore.

We had an applicant do that very thing. She was on SSI and told us it had to do with back problems. We verified SSI and took the application, but were unable to reach her previous or current landlord. Since there didn't seem to be anything wrong with her back, we suspected she had mental problems. When she started calling every ten minutes and hanging up, our suspicions were confirmed. Since she could afford the place, we insisted she would need to get a payee. She wouldn't hear of it and started pleading, begging and crying over the phone. "I pay my own rent," she kept saying. She did not say that she paid the rent on time, nor did she say we would never have to would never have to worry about receiving the rent. Thank goodness for voice mail, she continued to harass us for about a week and it finally stopped, presumably because someone else was stupid enough to rent to her.

Keep in mind, just because someone is on SSI doesn't mean they will pay the rent, and SSI money cannot be garnished.

Screening tenants can be very frustrating especially when quality applicants are few and far between. Checking out an application usually takes less than an hour IF people answer their phones and/or they call you back promptly. We have lost several tenants that probably would have been good, except while we were checking out their application and waiting for a call back, they found someplace else to live.

Think Positively

Even though we have lost a few good tenants, we have screened out a lot – and I mean a lot -- of potentially very bad tenants. In the long run, screening tenants will pay off. Better to lose a good tenant and have to wait for another one, than to rent to someone who you will end up having to evict after a few months. If more landlords started doing what we do, the quality of tenants would go up everywhere.

When tenants have to tell the truth on an application in order to get a place, when they have to show a track record of paying the rent on time, then it will become harder for the deadbeats to find a place to live. If you are thinking -- *where will those people live?* -- you are not giving them enough credit. You are in effect thinking they cannot raise themselves up to basic standards of normalcy, i.e. paying their rent like everyone else, you are doing them a huge disservice, and actually helping to keep them in poverty and negligent ways.

When more landlords raise their standards for their tenants, it will create a positive impact for everyone involved. By carefully screening tenants, you as a landlord could help change a rough neighborhood to a quiet one. You could even have an impact on children, helping them understand in order to afford a place to live, they need to be responsible citizens. By being diligent in the application process and choosing tenants, you are creating a path for success for your tenants and yourself.

Chapter Six

Whether to HUD or Not to HUD

The Housing Choice Voucher Program is Federal assistance provided by the US Department of Housing and Urban Development (HUD), and sponsors subsidized housing for low-income families and individuals. The program is more commonly known as Section 8 and usually referred to as HUD by tenants and landlords. Although Section 8 is a federal program, HUD is administered locally either by the city or the county. The program uses a voucher system for qualified applicants. A lot of landlords will not consider Section 8 for many reasons.

One of the advantages of Section 8 is you are guaranteed a *portion* of the rent. The tenant must pay their portion to stay on Section 8, and if the tenant is evicted they will not be able to be on the program again in that county or city for five years. Usually this is a strong motivator for tenants to pay their portion of the rent.

Read that very carefully again, not in *that particular city or county* for five years. The tenant can just go to another nearby jurisdiction and start Section 8 again.

When you have a house for rent, you will probably receive inquiries as to whether or not you accept HUD. If you do, and your prospective tenant likes your unit, you can have them fill out an application. When you decide to rent to the applicant, you will receive some paperwork to fill out which needs to be returned to the HUD office. The applicant will be responsible for this. HUD will require you to also fill out some forms and provide proof of ownership of that property. If you are purposely seeking HUD tenants, you can fill out the paperwork in advance and also have your rental on the HUD availability list.

Your property must qualify for HUD in two ways. First, the rent must be at fair market value. If you want to jack up the rent a couple of hundred dollars because of HUD, you will have to be able to show that surrounding rentals collect similar amounts. Also, HUD has already given the qualified applicant a maximum rent they will allow, which turns out to be close to the average rent in lower income areas.

The property must also pass a HUD inspection. Once your applicant turns in the paperwork to the case worker, you will be contacted to set a time for the inspection. Someone will have to be at the house in order to let the inspector inside. You will not know that day whether or not it passed. A few days later you will receive a letter as to whether the property passed or failed. If the property failed, the letter will explain what needs to be repaired and by what date. If you decide not to do the repairs, you will have to find another non-Section 8 tenant. After you complete the repairs, the inspector will come back and check only those items.

Once you have approved a tenant, it may take a month or more before they can move in. The tenant is responsible for the deposit.

If you are seeking HUD tenants and are already listed at the local housing office, you can arrange for the inspection to be done in advance. That way when the tenant you want comes along, the house has already been approved. There may be a fee for this.

Every year your unit or house will have to pass an HUD inspection. Once the property has passed the initial inspection, it usually passes subsequent inspections fairly easily unless the tenant has incurred some damage or new guidelines have been implemented by the county.

You will put the HUD tenant on your lease, but there is also a one year lease that you and the tenant must sign for government administrative purposes.

Overall, the process is not too cumbersome and we used to be proponents of Section 8. One of the benefits of Section 8 is that older HUD tenants and those on disabilities seem to be relatively stable and stay for a long time.

Nevertheless, we will no longer accept Section 8.

Not long ago we were talking to a fellow property owner. He owns several apartment buildings in another city. Many of the tenants in his apartment were on HUD and he thought it was a great program. We told him we no longer took Section 8 and explained why. He said he never had any problems like we experienced. As luck would have it, several months later he called and told us, he would not be renewing any of his HUD tenants either.

So what's the problem?

Tenants Don't Understand or Try and Cheat the System

Section 8 works as follows. Once someone qualifies for Section 8, they will receive a voucher that will indicate the number of bedrooms they qualify to rent. The voucher will give them a rent amount that HUD will allow. Usually this allowance is based upon the current market rent in the area HUD is servicing. The amount is more than enough for a tenant to find an apartment and sometimes enough for a small house. A small house that will fit within HUD guidelines will be an older home in a lower income neighborhood. HUD does not allow their recipients to live in upper end housing unless the landlord is willing to substantially reduce their rent.

Let's say the voucher allows the recipient to have a three bedroom that rents for $700. You happen to have a three bedroom that you are renting for $650. You go, "Yippie skippie, I can get $50 more a month if I take Section 8!"

Not so fast, also included in the voucher is an allowance for electric, water, and gas; meaning HUD is going to deduct the average utility fees from what you can get for rent. If HUD deems the average utility charge will be about $150 a month, you can ask $550 from HUD for your house.

As long as all you wanted for your rental was $550 anyway, the Section 8 system works. But often the landlord will have to lower rent in order to bring in a HUD tenant. In our opinion, Section 8 doesn't offer enough incentive to lower your rent for one of their recipients.

Now remember, Section 8 is only paying a *portion* of the tenant's rent, so the tenant will have to come up with their part. The tenant's portion will vary according to whatever income the Section 8 recipient receives. HUD has looked at their income and determined exactly what amount each party will pay.

Let's say you're renting your house for $550 and the tenant qualifies for $700 place with $150 allowance for utilities. You will not receive a $550 check from HUD. You will receive a portion of the rent from HUD and a portion of the rent from the tenant. This amount has been prearranged. Possibly HUD will only pay $200 and you will need to collect $250 from your tenant. In this case, Section 8 is not even guaranteeing half the rent amount. Other times, HUD may guarantee $500 and you only need to collect $50 from the tenant. Before accepting someone who is on Section 8, carefully consider the amount that HUD will guarantee. The last thing you want is a who can't or won't pay their portion, and Section 8 is only contributing a small fraction of the rent due.

HUD recipients do not fully understand the rules regarding their portion of the rent. They generally believe they qualify for anyplace that is $700 or less, not realizing the place needs to meet certain HUD standards. If you are unaware of HUD qualifications and rely on what the prospective tenant tells you, you may be in for some unpleasant surprises. You could agree to rent to someone only to find out HUD will not qualify your home causing a prolonged vacancy.

Let's go back to the house that should rent for $650. Even though HUD will only allow the applicant $500, we have had applicants say they would happily pay the $150 difference. When a prospective tenant does that, they are cheating the government, even though some are sincere that this is perfectly okay. It is not okay, it is illegal and if caught could cause you serious legal problems, fines, and possibly jail time.

Another way HUD tenants will cheat the system is to bring other people in to live with them. We had one HUD tenant who was supposed to be living in the unit with her grandson. The child's mother was in prison and the father had disappeared, so grandma had custody. Her husband had recently died and she didn't have any income. So far, everything was legitimate. Then the grandmother started dating a fairly wealthy man and after awhile moved in with him while still claiming to be living in the unit. She allowed her adult son (the child's uncle) to stay at the rental unit who benefitted from reduced rent. The tenant knew what she was doing was illegal, and we knew she was breaking the law. We communicated our concerns to her Section 8 caseworker and were told we would have to prove any allegations – expensive and difficult.

Another time a young lady and her fiancé applied to rent one of the houses we were managing. She was on Section 8 and claimed she would be living there by herself with her little boy. However, she and her fiancé both filled out the application. It was a tip-off, he was going to be living there with her. Next!

Inspections and Re-Inspections

It used to be that Section 8 inspections were fairly routine and the inspectors looked for basic items that any reasonable landlord would fix anyway. The inspectors were very particular that hot water heaters have a stream release valve, which are already installed in newer models, and fairly easy to put in on the older ones. Carpet and linoleum must be tacked or glued down so people won't trip, screens must be on windows, light switches must work along with the appliances that the landlord is providing with the home. Reasonable enough.

Around the year 2000, the inspections changed. Inspectors started looking at more than just health and safety. Rental units had to be up to code. Sounds okay, right?

What is critical to understand about the inspections is this: No matter what the building codes where when the house was constructed and no matter what improvements you made to the house, Section 8 will evaluate the house at the current year building codes.

As previously mentioned, only lower income properties will financially qualify for HUD, which tend to be older homes. If you have an older home or apartment you are renting for Section 8, do not be surprised when just about your entire house will fail the inspection. Guess who is responsible to fix all the repairs—the landlord. If the repairs are done to the inspector's satisfaction, your property is ready for a Section 8 tenant.

Now calculate, how much time and money did you spend getting the house ready for Section 8? In most cases you could have already had a qualified tenant paying the rent with a fraction of the repair cost.

Some of the repairs HUD now requires are as follows and come from actual HUD inspections:

- Electrical plugs must be grounded. However, the inspector only looks to see if it is a 3-pronged plug and doesn't know if it has actually been grounded or not.

- Every wall must have a plug. Unfortunately, many older homes do not have outlets on every wall.

For example, we managed an older home where the outside walls were made of concrete blocks. It was a well-built sturdy house, but none of the exterior made from the blocks had outlets. There were plenty of plugs on the other walls, but HUD would not consider the house because electrical outlets were not on every single wall. No exceptions.

We managed an older home that was freshly painted and newly carpeted. It was a cute little house. There was nothing wrong with it, yet a HUD inspection came up with three pages of repairs. *Three pages!* What were the terrible things wrong with the house? Being an older building, it didn't have a top shelf in the closets, this is a HUD requirement. The house had one of those old fashioned mail slots in the front door. The mail slot was considered a hole in the wall and needed to be repaired.

The old electrical fuse box had been switched over to a circuit breaker; however the fuse box – no longer in use -- was still in the wall and had a couple of missing fuses. Well it didn't matter that the house had been converted to a circuit breaker and was no longer using fuses; HUD was insistent that fuses be put in that box. The kitchen cabinets did not have knobs, HUD insisted on knobs. The *detached* garage had some holes in the walls, those had to be fixed, although no one was going to be living or sleeping in the garage. The tenant's child had marked on the wall, and made a dirty spot on the carpet and it was *our* job to clean up, not the tenant's.

We told the tenant, we weren't going to do all these silly repairs. She volunteered to make the repairs at no charge to us, and so we went ahead and rented to her.

We thought maybe this inspection was a fluke, but in another unit when it came time for re-inspection, the HUD inspector found a dirty oven. The unit didn't pass because of a dirty oven? HUD wanted us to clean the tenant's dirty oven. The answer to that was, NO -- either the tenant cleans it or the tenant moves. Rather than clean the dirty oven that the tenant herself created, she moved.

Section 8 Lease Takes Priority

When you go with HUD, you will have two leases. The lease between you and the tenant, and the year lease between you, the tenant and HUD. If there is a problem with your lease, too bad, the HUD lease will take priority. This means, if you have something in your lease that you require the tenant to do or not to do, but it is not addressed in the HUD lease, there is nothing you can do about it. If they are parking 20 cars on the front lawn and HUD doesn't care, too bad. If your Section 8 tenant is paying the rent, the only thing you can do is not renew with the at the end of the year. But in the meantime, you're stuck with their noise, their trash, and their crummy behavior.

We were told that if the HUD tenant left the place trashed, HUD will help defray some of the fix-up costs that went beyond the deposit. It only seemed right. Section 8 puts you through hoops to provide a place that is clean and to their standards when a tenant moves in; if their tenant trashes the place, HUD should help pay the costs and go after the tenant for reimbursement. If that was truly ever the case, it is not anymore. Section 8's attitude is, "take it out of the deposit." Of course, many states have capped how much a landlord can ask for a deposit and inevitably the deposit doesn't cover all the repairs.

Evictions

The one thing Section 8 is fairly good at, is making the tenant pay their share of the rent. They will discuss the ramifications of non-payment to their tenant and threaten them with being kicked out of the program if there is an eviction. If you are dealing with a normal tenant, they will usually make their portion of the sub-sidized rent a priority. However, threats and/or reason will mean absolutely nothing to those tenants who are mentally ill or addicted to drugs.

If your tenant doesn't pay the rent, you can at least evict. During the time of non-payment from the tenant you will still be receiving the portion from HUD. We had to do one HUD eviction. The tenant had been a fairly good payer for awhile, but then she got strung-out on drugs. First came the lies and the late rent, then she didn't pay at all. She had to go. We tried working with her and calling her caseworker, all to no avail.

So we evicted her. Naturally, she trashed the place. It cost around $3000 to make it rent ready again, much more than her deposit. Then Section 8 had the nerve to tell us we owed them some back rent because the tenant was not at the property for the entire month when she was evicted.

That was the final straw. We no longer take new HUD tenants. If Section 8 works for you, great. In fact, we have had some very good, long-term tenants on HUD. Remember, you are not obligated to take Section 8 and neither are you obligated to re-new once their lease is up.

How HUD Screwed Everybody

We were trying to rent a two bedroom apartment in Sacramento, and not having a lot of luck getting qualified tenants. We held an open house and collected a few applications that didn't seem promising. As we were leaving a woman and her son drove up. She was on HUD. We still liked HUD at the time and she fit our profile of a perfect tenant. An older woman on HUD tends to pay the rent and doesn't go anywhere.

Her application checked out and we told her we would rent to her. We followed the same process we always followed with HUD, and based on the paperwork, her initial deposit and portion of the rent we let her move in understanding HUD would pay nothing until after the unit passed inspection.

Once the paperwork goes back to HUD, they will schedule an inspection. Neither the tenant or ourselves received a call to schedule an inspection; nor did we receive HUD's portion of the check even though all the required paperwork had been done. We spoke to the tenant and she didn't understand it either. Her case-worker had told her it was okay to move and her unit would be approved. The rent was definitely within the HUD guidelines as to what they would pay.

We tried calling the local HUD office to see what was going on, and could only listen to recorded instructions to press this button, more instructions, hold, leave a message. Naturally, no one ever called us back.

Fortunately our tenant, who we found out was on dialysis two times a week, had a direct number for her caseworker. Of course, when we called, we still had to leave a message and she never returned our calls.

Another month went by. The tenant was dutifully paying her portion of the rent, but nothing from HUD. We weren't too worried because once this was straightened out, HUD would pay for the back rent. Then the tenant called and told us the inspector would be out. Okay, good. The inspector never came. It turned out, he went to the old place where she had been living, and the HUD checks were still going there.

Finally, we were able to speak to the tenant's caseworker. She was very rude and curt with us, "Mrs. G. didn't have the authority to move," and she hung up the phone.

We told the tenant about the problem, but she had no more control than we did. However, we needed full payment of the rent, and told her she needed to pay the full amount or leave. She was too poor to pay the full amount, so she had to leave. It turned out there was a problem with the number of bedrooms she was living in. She qualified for a one bedroom, but our place had two bedrooms even though our rent was still low enough to be within the one-bedroom HUD guidelines. So what was the problem? The tenant's health problems were severe enough that her doctor allowed her to have a live-in person to help her do things. Rather than have a stranger move in, she wanted it to be her son. For some reason, HUD didn't approve of that living situation.

We no choice but to insist Mrs. G. move and she went to live with her daughter. Six months later, HUD finally straightened out the situation, and Mrs. G. called us wondering if she could move back. By then, we had the place rented to someone else.

Chapter Seven

The Lease

You can go to practically any office supply store and purchase rental agreement forms. Usually, these are one or two pages and probably won't cover every issue you need to protect yourself and your property. You may decide to hire a lawyer draw up a lease. If you are a member of the Board of Realtors®, you can use their standard rental agreement. In most states it is legal to create your own lease. You can go online and discover many providers of leases for your state. Which way you go is up to you. However, always use a written lease.

Many of the items you might include in your lease and why are discussed in this chapter. You probably don't want to incorporate all of the elements, otherwise your lease will end up being twenty pages long and that's enough to scare away even the best tenant.

Check with your state to see what is and is not allowed in a lease. For instance, many states will let you collect attorney and court costs in case of an eviction. Alabama, however, will not. Judges may invalidate the entire lease if an unsuspecting landlord has attorney fees or other disallowed clauses in the contract. If you are uncertain, have an attorney help you create a readable and understandable lease.

This chapter explains many of the components you should consider putting into your lease. As with all the information in this book, nothing written here should be construed as legal advice, and we strongly advise that you consult with an attorney regarding any questions and issues about creating a lease.

Tenant's Name and the Landlord's Name

It is important which names you use, because that is who you are going to have to sue for eviction and fix-up costs. Make sure all names are spelled correctly and that tenants are of legal age and competent to sign. Check the prospective tenant's driver's license to confirm age and ensure they are who they say they are.

Premises

Specify the exact address where the tenant is renting.

Rent, Deposit and How Paid

Usually the lease will serve as the receipt for the tenant's deposit and first month's rent payment. You need to put in the monthly rent amount, and how it is to be paid: mailed, picked up, delivered to office, or put directly into the bank.

Late Fees

In most states, unless you specify what day the rent is due, the tenant has the entire month to pay the rent. You want the tenant to be clear that the rent is due on the first and late on whatever date you pick – usually a three to five day grace period. The problem with the grace period is most tenants wait until that day to pay their rent.

Some states have put a cap on late fees, so find out what your state allows. We have heard of some landlords who have graduating late fees, like $2 per day. We have a fixed late fee, around ten percent of the rent, because if the tenant hasn't paid by the due date and hasn't called, we're starting the eviction anyway.

Term

This tells when the lease begins and whether it will be month to month, six months, or a year lease. We always do month to month for very good reasons. If you have a tenant you want out because they complain all the time, on a month to month, you simply need to give them thirty day notice to vacate and you're done. However, if you signed a year lease, you are stuck with them until the end of the term.

On a month to month lease, won't the good tenants leave earlier? Not usually. There seems to be a psychology with tenants who have been locked into a year's lease. The minute the year is up, they want to move. Why? No particular reason except, they are now free to do so without penalty. When they are free to leave by simply giving a thirty day notice, tenants tend to stay longer.

Because we do month to month leases, and are looking for long-term tenants, during the application process, we ask how long they plan to live on the premises. If the applicants indicate they are a short termers, we decide how badly we want them – which usually isn't very bad.

Security Deposit

Some states have created limits as to how much security deposit you can ask for, but one month's rent is usually the standard amount. With borderline tenants we will ask for two month's worth of security deposit, if the state will allow that much. In many areas it is commonplace to ask for first and last month's rent plus a deposit.

When a state limits the amount of deposit you can collect, see if the state will allow a non-refundable risk liability fee. The nice thing about such a fee, is you don't have to pay it back.

Check with the laws in your state to see exactly how to handle security deposits. Some states require that you hold the deposit in an interest bearing account. Explain in the lease how security deposits will be handled.

Possession

Possession is basically a statement saying that the tenant will be allowed to possess the house until the term expires at which time, the tenant will agree to peaceably give up the premises to the landlord in as good condition as when delivered, ordinary wear and tear excepted. In this section, you may also include a statement that the tenants will keep the landlord updated with a current phone number where they can be contacted.

Use of Premises/Absence

You may want to include the obvious that the rental is to be a dwelling only. If the tenant is going to be gone for an extended length of time, the tenant agrees to notify the landlord. In this clause, you might state whether or not the tenant may also use the premises for an in-home business and the type of business. Make sure the tenant's in-home business complies with local zoning laws.

You may also add that the tenant will not have illegal substances on the property. Naturally this statement is no guarantee your tenant will not turn your property into a meth-house or a center of prostitution, but this clause helps protect you that you are not condoning such activities. If you believe your property is vulnerable to this type of activity, consult with your attorney for other precautions you can take to protect your investment.

Occupants

Some portion of the lease should include a list of all the people who will be living in the house whether or not they are helping pay the rent. You will include names of the tenant's roommates and children. If there are a total of five people in the family, you may want to start it out : No more than five (5) person(s) may reside at ADDRESS, and list their names.

A rule of thumb for deciding maximum occupancy is two people per bedroom. It is preferable not to allow children over five years old of different genders to share the same bedroom. Some states have codified how many occupants are allowed per room.

In theory, if the tenant brings another occupant in without permission you can require the tenant to remove the occupant or move. Proving others are actually living there is difficult, but it is still good to have occupant information on the lease.

Pets

If tenants have pets, charge a pet deposit per animal in addition to the normal rent deposit. Some landlords will require the tenant to pay an extra ten or twenty dollars more a month for "pet rent."

Destructive pets are not good, but it is very hard for tenants with destructive pets to find places to live -- impetus for them to pay the rent and not complain. If their pet is peeing all over the carpet, but the tenant doesn't care and they stay longer than the life of the carpet...who cares. If the tenant moves out and the place is a disaster, suck it up, clean it up and sue the tenant for the repairs. Remember, you have rented to someone who has a steady job and an income that can be garnished.

Quiet Enjoyment

Here is where you tell the tenant how much notice you are going to give them before inspecting or entering the premises, which will be determined by the laws in your state. Most states require twenty-four hour notice or more before entering unless it is an emergency situation. The clause has nothing to do with ensuring that the tenant's neighbors will be quiet and leave them alone. You may have to explain that to your new tenant.

Furnishings

When you are providing items on the property, you need to list them. Some of these items might be a refrigerator, stove, draperies. You do not need to include items that are attached to the property such as a hot water heater (attached by pipes) or drapery rods. Naturally, if you are providing a furnished unit, you will need to list every piece of furniture, wall hangings and lamps. Taking "before" pictures is a good idea whether you are providing furnishings or not. Sometimes tenants will remove fixtures -- items attached to the property -- like a chandelier or cabinets.

Property Insurance

This is an explanation of what insurance you will cover and what insurance you won't. You will generally carry dwelling insurance which will cover fire and wind damage to the property. Usually your insurance will not cover any damage caused by your tenant. Neither will it cover any of the tenant's possessions. If tenants want their possessions insured, they need to obtain renter's insurance. You can include a statement saying you are not to be held responsible for any loss or damage that may happen to their possessions.

Keys

The number of keys and type of keys you are giving the tenant is listed in this clause. If the keys are not returned there will be a charge for this, often based on the cost of rekeying.

In many apartments and in some neighborhoods, the mail goes into a locked mailbox. The Post Office usually charges a fee to obtain a mailbox key, and some postal workers get a little prickly when having the re-key the box when a new tenant moves in. Sometimes the post office makes it difficult for the tenant to obtain a key. You can go ahead and pay for the key yourself, and charge a separate deposit for the mailbox key. If the key is returned, you can return their deposit and give the key to the next tenant. If the key is not returned, you're not out any money.

Lockout

To avoid phone calls in the middle of the night from a drunk tenant who can't find their keys, we charge a $200 fee to regain entry to the rental. A steep charge makes it cheaper for the tenant to call a locksmith, or break in themselves and repair the window at their cost rather than to bother us. We have never had to open a door for a tenant because of a lost key.

Condition of Premises

The condition of premises clause speaks to everything in the rental both inside and out. The tenant has three days to notify you of any problems, otherwise the property is said to be in a workable, usable and habitable condition at the time of moving in. When it comes to plumbing stoppages and clogs, this clause is extremely handy. If three days go by and the tenant hasn't brought any repairs or problems with the property to your attention, then the tenant received a house with clear plumbing and any stoppage was caused by them and they need to pay for it. Broken windows, doors, screens on the windows and a host of other things, will be covered under this clause. Photographs provide additional proof about the condition of the house.

Maintenance

You need to put in writing what you will repair and what your tenant will be responsible for. If there you have a yard and you expect the tenant to care for it, you must put in the lease that the tenant agrees to mow, fertilize, and water the lawn. Many cities have weed ordinances and will fine the owner – not the tenant -- if the weeds get too high. Addressing yard work in the lease will save you from becoming your tenant's monthly yard maintenance worker.

Here are some other items you might want to include that your tenant will be need to follow:

- Not to block sidewalks, hallways, driveways, stairs etc.

- Keep windows, doors, locks, etc. in good, clean order and repair.

- Not to obstruct windows and doors.

- Not to leave doors and windows open in inclement weather.

- Not to install locks or hooks on doors and windows without permission.

- Keep heat and air conditioning filters clean. Why should you have to change their air filters? And you can charge the tenant for the service call if a heat/air technician determines all they needed to do was change the filter.

- Keep sinks, toilet and all other plumbing in good order and repair. This again speaks to stoppages and leaks.

- Tenants, family and guests on premises will not participate in illegal activities or bring illegal substances on the property.

- Keep TV's stereos turned down so as not to disturb other tenants or neighbors.

- Deposit trash, rubbish in proper location.

- To be present and allow a service provider to enter the premises and make the required repairs. If a service provider is not able to enter at the agreed upon time, the tenant will pay $100 for each occurrence. You will still have the pay a service charge whether or not the tenant is there, so pass this cost onto the tenant and some extra for your trouble. If landlord must be present for service provider, the tenant will pay $50 for each occurrence.

- Pay the rent, regardless repairs being completed. Although in most states it is law that the tenant must pay rent regardless of whether the landlord does repairs, it is a good idea to reiterate this in the lease. Most repairs are not emergencies and sometimes it takes a service provider a few days to come out. If the provider has to order a part to repair an older appliance, it can take a couple of more days for the part to arrive. In the meantime, if the tenant is getting impatient and feeling put out, too bad. That's life, they still have to pay rent.

- Comply with building and housing codes.

Landlord's Rules and Regulations

If you are going to have your own rules and regulations like "no smoking" in your house, then you need to add this.

Parking

You will need a parking clause in your lease if you are renting out a place that has a designated parking area. State exactly where the tenant can park, include a diagram if necessary. To avoid tenants parking cars in the back or front yard, you can might specify parking should be in the driveway, garage and on the street only.

Storage

Like the parking, you can limit where a tenant can store their belongs. Basically, you want the tenant to store their things in the house and not outside where other people can see a bunch of ugly boxes.

Alterations and Repairs

Include a statement that says the tenant will not perform any alterations or repairs to the property without receiving your written permission. We allow tenants to paint and even use bright, bold interior colors if that is what they like. The only specification is they bring the walls back to the original color when they move.

Utilities/Services

Explain in your lease what utilities you are paying and what the tenant is paying. In single family homes, the tenant pays for all utilities. In duplexes and multi-units the landlord is usually responsible for water, sewer and trash. If the units are not separately metered, the landlord may need to pay all the utilities including gas and electric.

Waterbeds

Waterbeds seem to be a relic of the past, but it might be good to prohibit them in the lease just in case. The problem with water-beds is that they are heavy and prone to leaking. If the house is vandalized and the waterbed slashed, there will be enough water released to destroy the carpet and warp the flooring. The tenant can have a waterbed if they are willing to purchase waterbed insurance and name you as the beneficiary.

Hazardous Materials

Here is a statement that will prohibit the tenant from bringing hazardous materials on the premises, although you probably wouldn't know it if they did. However, it will help protect you in case your tenant does something crazy like storing kegs of gunpowder in the house, or makes pesticides in the bathtub.

Compliance with Regulations

The tenant agrees to abide by all laws federal, state, county, local, ordinances, regulations and everything else. You may want to add a specific sentence regarding illegal drugs and have them initial that part. The clause is to prove that you the landlord are doing due diligence on the war on drugs and you can show in writing you are not tolerating substance abuse on your property.

Lead Based Paint

On residential properties built before 1978, Federal law requires a lead based paint disclosure. After 1978, lead based paint was no longer used, so this disclosure is not necessary. You can go to the EPA website and download this disclosure.

Taxes

Landlord pays property taxes.

Habitability

The tenant agrees to give the landlord reasonable notice if the habitability of the premises have changed.

Defaults

If tenant doesn't comply with the terms of the lease, your default clause spells out what the landlord will do to remedy the situation. Usually, the tenant will be given a notice to fix the problem within a specific time period, and if not, face eviction.

Posting Fees

Include in your lease what you are going to charge your tenant if you have to start eviction or other legal proceedings against them. Most states require that if tenants do not pay the rent -- and/or fix, or adhere to other items in the lease -- you must give them written notice. Sometimes you must deliver this notice in person, often you can simply post it on the tenant's main entryway. Regardless, when you have to post for some kind of infraction, the tenant should pay for your time and trouble. Make sure your state doesn't have any prohibitions against charging these types of fees.

We always include posting fees of $50 or more in the lease to help defray our cost and time. If a property is located too far away for us to post a notice, we will have to hire someone – usually a process server – to do the job for us. This can be expensive and tenants should pay for their own negligence.

Holdover

If the tenant says they are going to be out on a certain date and remains longer, then they must pay the rent as agreed to in the lease. The additional rent is usually pro-rated and charged per diem.

Non-Sufficient Funds

This deals with the problem of bounced checks. We add at least $10 to what the bank charges us for depositing a bounced check. If the tenant fails to make good on the bad check, we still start the eviction proceedings and file the bad check with the local district attorney. After a tenant bounces a check, we will only take cash or certified funds as payment thereafter.

Cumulative Rights

You need a statement in the lease that says if you and the tenant agree to something either verbally or in writing outside the purview of the lease or agree to make changes to some parts of the lease, this agreement doesn't negate the rest of the lease. The reason for this is that judges have been known to invalidate an entire contract when such instances occur. For example, maybe the rent is due on the third and you agree to take it on the fifth without charging a late fee. You want to ensure that your verbal agreement doesn't end up invalidating the rest of the lease. However, if you make changes to the lease, better to put it in writing and have your tenant sign. Especially if you created your own lease without the benefit of an attorney, it would be wise to include a proviso that says if a court rules that part of the lease is unenforceable that doesn't make the rest of the lease void, only the part that was found unenforceable.

Indemnification

You want to include the standard legal clause that holds the landlord harmless for anything and everything.

Assignability/Subletting

You may want to include a sentence that says the tenant cannot sell, sublet or assign the lease to someone else. This clause is more pertinent in rent control areas. A tenant may have been living in a rent controlled unit for many years and is now paying hundreds of dollars below market rent and decide to move. Rather than give up their apartment, they could rent it to someone at the market rent, hoping make a little profit for themselves. Nope. The landlord works too hard for the tenant to profit off of under-market rents. In addition the new tenant becomes your problem.

Neighborhood Conditions

Because you as a landlord usually have no idea who the neighbors are and what conditions exist there; you might add a statement that makes the tenant responsible to determine what the neighborhood is like. That way if it turns out the house is in a high crime neighborhood, right under a flight path, downwind from a sewage treatment facility, or the rental is next door to flagrant drug dealers, the tenant doesn't have recourse that you failed to mention these issues to them.

Megan's Law

Some states require you put in the lease the website where tenants may go to find out about registered sexual offenders.

Military Ordinance

If your property is located within the parameters of a former or current military installation, for your protection you may want to include a clause informing the tenant of this fact. There could be leftover ordinance like an unexploded grenade that could cause potential harm. Another example might be a military arsenal that could become a future superfund site.

Methamphetamine

In some states you must disclose if you know your rental was contaminated by methamphetamine.

Signs

You might include a statement that allows you to put up a FOR SALE sign while the tenant is still living on the property. You can still put one up without this clause, but the tenant may claim it is in their right to take it back down.

Tenant Estoppels

If you are selling the property, the new owner will want to verify how much rent the tenants are paying. The buyer's tendency will be think you might be overstating how much rent you are receiving. A statement in your lease will obligate the tenant to sign the disclosure as long as it is true.

Tenant's Obligation Upon Vacating

In this clause you can specify exactly how you want the tenant to leave the property. You can include items like all the doors and windows are to be closed and locked, the unit and surrounding areas free from trash, and all pets and personal items are to be removed from the premises.

Damage To Premises

Some leases specify what will happen to the tenant if they damage the premises. Be careful here not to make the consequences too intimidating and scare away a good tenant.

Early Termination

When your tenant is on a year lease, you will need to explain what the consequences will be if the tenant vacates before the term ends. Your remedy will vary according to state. Usually you can sue for lost rent, but must make a concerted effort to rent the property within a reasonable time period. If you re-rent the property right away, you cannot claim lost rent until the end of the former occupant's term, only the rent for the amount of time the property was vacant. Note, we have found putting all our tenants on a month to month tenancy makes life easier for everyone.

Temporary Relocation

One reason for a temporary relocation would be if you have to fumigate the rental and the tenants will have to go away for awhile. Flooding from a burst pipe might be another reason the tenant will have to temporarily vacate. For this type of occurrence, a temporary relocation clause indicating the tenant will not have to pay rent during their absence but the landlord will not be responsible for the tenant's motel or other living expenses during this period could help prevent a lawsuit.

Mediation

If there is a dispute between you and the tenant, rather than running to court and filing a lawsuit, you will first agree to mediation. If mediation doesn't work, you will go to binding arbitration. Think long and hard about including a mediation clause, as mediators and arbitrators can be more expensive than going to court. In many states, you cannot appeal an arbitrator's ruling.

Attorney Fees

The tenant agrees to pay attorney fees and court costs if you have to go to court against your tenant for any reason. Some states do *not* allow landlords to charge attorney's fees. If that is the case, keep this clause out of your lease.

Foreign Language Negotiation

Some states require that if the rental agreement was negotiated in a foreign language, the lease must also be written in that same language. If you are dealing with someone who is from a foreign country, you may have them write something like: English is not my native language, but I read and understand English perfectly. Have them write it themselves and initial the statement. Doing so, will protect you from tenants who pretend in court they don't understand English and claim they didn't understand what they were signing.

Guarantee

You only need this when you have a co-signer. The person who is the guaranteeing the lease will not be living at the property, but are guaranteeing the rent will be paid. You can go after them rather than the tenant for rent and claims against the lease.

Sign and Date

Of course, all tenants named on the lease must sign and date it as well as you the landlord. They need a copy with your signature, and you need a copy with their signatures.

Remember, the lease is designed primarily to protect you and your property. You want a tough lease that is defendable in a court of law yet flexible enough to give you leeway to work with your tenants in a friendly manner. The specifics in the lease will need to reflect local and state laws. If you have an attorney draw up your lease, read it carefully all the way through and make sure you understand everything written and there is no ambiguity. Ambiguity makes for problems that need to be interpreted by a judge – which means more money out of your pocket to pay your attorney. What's more, if you don't understand your own lease, how can you expect tenants to abide by it and how can you enforce it?

Chapter Eight

Giving Away the Keys

Okay, so you've prepared the lease and set a time to meet the tenants to sign and give them access to the property. When you call your new tenants, tell them how much money to bring with them and tell them it must be in *cash or certified funds*.

No checks!

Assure your new tenants that next month, they will be able to give you a check if they prefer, but never, ever let someone into a property without verifiable funds. Also, never let a tenant in if they do not bring the full amount agreed upon. Finally, retain the keys until the tenants have signed the lease.

When signing the lease, do not have the tenant come to your home. Bring two copies of the lease with you, one for yourself and one for the tenant and meet them either at the property or at a nearby coffee shop to finalize the lease. Letting your new tenants go through the rental one last time before signing is usually a good idea. They will probably have some last minute questions.

Sometimes, however, those last minute questions become last minute demands. If they have not yet signed the lease, call their bluff and ask if they really want the place. Better to lose a tenant at the last minute than to have one who is constantly whining or refuses to pay the rent because the property doesn't measure up to their standards.

Let your soon-to-be tenants read through the lease and answer any questions they might have. You can have them initial every page if you wish, and if there are items of special importance to you, you can have them initial beside those. Most tenants will browse through and sign. Some will read every word.

Every person named on the lease should sign the lease.

Before you sign the lease, count the rent and deposit money. Your lease can serve as the receipt.

It is not necessary for the tenants to sign their copy of the lease. Just make sure you leave with the copy that the tenants signed.

Rent Collection Methods

While going over the lease, is the time to explain how you are will collect the rent. Allowing your tenant to mail you a check is a poor way to collect rent. Tenants will often tell you "the check is in the mail," just to stall off an eviction. Claiming their check is lost in the mail is a handy excuse to avoid late charges. If you decide to have the tenants mail checks, set up a post office box rather than reveal your home address.

A lot of tenants, especially those living in low cost rentals, need someone to come by each month and collect rent in person. In fact, we had one tenant who would call us on Friday evening after he was paid to come pick up the rent. If we did not arrive at his place within the hour, he had the money spent already – not one of our better tenants.

One of the nice things about picking up rent, is you have a reason to go by and inspect the property every month. You also have an opportunity you to peek on the inside and see how the tenants are taking care of the interiors. If you use the pick-up-the rent-in-person method, call the tenant beforehand to tell them you are coming and ensure they actually have the rent. If you prefer not to pick up the rent in person, but you have tenants who cannot get rent paid any other way, consider including a small fee for the service, especially if you stop by and they are not home.

Unless you are a real estate agent and have a brokerage office, do not have tenants drop off the rent where you work. Neither should tenants come to you home to pay the rent. Your tenants don't need to know where you live. Keeping your home address undisclosed to tenants is not just about privacy and safety. There is a jealousy factor. Your tenants already think you have all kinds of money. If they see your home is three times the size of theirs, they won't believe you if they want a new carpet and you say you can't afford it at this time.

We have found the most efficient way to handle rent collection is for tenants to go directly to the bank and deposit the funds in your rental account. Don't panic, you're not giving them your personal banking account number. Using a minimum deposit in a checking or savings, set up a rental checking account at a bank with a branch near the tenant's home. Give the tenant the bank's name and the account number. The tenant can go to the bank and deposit the rent directly into your rental account. In fact, the tenant doesn't even need to fill out a deposit slip, merely show the account number to the teller and hand over the rent. The bank teller will give your tenant a receipt and you don't have to run by their house and beg for money, neither do you have to listen to their lies that the check is in the mail.

Here's how to handle your rental accounts. Set up one account per rental property for two reasons. If two or more tenants share an account, you will not know who paid especially if they put in a partial payment or their rent is the same. Also, if you need to start an eviction, you can close out one account without affecting the other tenants.

For convenience, monitor your bank accounts on-line.

At the first of the month, simply go on-line and see if the tenant paid. Most banks will show immediately when a deposit has been entered. Some old fashioned banks still have a lag time, and the deposit for rent may not show until the next business day.

Checks will usually show the same day of deposit, but funds may not be available for a few days.

If the tenant has not paid by the day specified in the lease, the following day you can post a notice to pay or quit. Once the rent money is in the account, you can pay the mortgage and other bills directly from that account or you can transfer the funds to a master account.

Pro-Rated Rent and Deposits

When dealing with lower income tenants, coming up with a deposit is very difficult for them. We used to work with people to help with this situation by taking take half the deposit and a hundred extra per month until the deposit was paid. This rarely worked. The tenants would get into the property and never pay the rest of the deposit. Then when they left, the small deposit they paid wouldn't take care of the cleaning and repairs.

If you are willing to work with someone to get into the property, insist on receiving the entire deposit and instead negotiate with the first month's rent. Perhaps you've noticed signs around large apartment complexes that say, "First Month Rent Free." You'll never see a sign inviting people to rent without paying a deposit. The reason is tenants need some "skin in the game," and a refundable deposit fulfills that purpose.

Tenants need to have the idea they can get all their deposit back when they leave. A partial deposit is not going to be enough motivation for them to leave the place rent-ready. But a deposit return for an entire month's rent or more becomes quite an incentive. Therefore work with the tenant on the first month's rent but insist on a deposit.

On the other hand, think twice about foregoing the first month's rent in order to get a tenant into your rental. We have seen time and time again, if the prospective tenants cannot come up with rent *and* deposit, they really can't afford the place. Only if consider taking a reduced first month's rent if you property has been vacant for a long time.

When a property needs some cleaning and minor fix-up, tenants are sometimes willing to do the work for you. You can deduct the sweat-equity off the first month's rent and collect the full deposit. When a tenant does the work themselves on a property, they seem to have a sense of pride and want to retain possession of the property.

Ask for a copy of all the receipts the tenant paid and make arrangements to inspect the property. On the lease indicate the move-in provision that you made: One month rent off to bring the property to rent ready condition. If the tenant leaves the place a mess, or never did the work promised, keep the deposit.

Tenants who move in during the middle of the month, will need to pay pro-rated for the month. Try to collect the deposit and the next month's rent along with the pro-rated rent for the current month. For example, if the tenant is moving into the property in the middle of February, collect deposit, March's rent, and the pro-rated rent for February. The next rent due will be in April.

If the tenant cannot afford this, see if you can get next month's full rent when signing the lease, and at the beginning of the month collect the first month's pro-rated rent. In this case you would collect deposit and full month's rent in the middle of February, and in March the tenant would pay you pro-rated rent.

Only after the tenants have paid you all the deposit and rent, do you give them a key. You only need to give them one key for each exterior lock; they can make their own copies.

Once you have the funds, the copy of the lease signed by the tenants, and you have given away the key, you are done...at least for awhile.

Don't be surprised if you get a few phone calls from the tenants in the next day or so. They may have questions about the house, or there may be some repairs that only became evident when someone moved in. Houses that have been sitting for awhile with the utilities off, usually have plumbing issues, and that is not the new tenant's fault. Get someone out right away to take care of these problems.

Perception Becomes Reality

Because you are a property owner and a landlord, your tenants will perceive you as someone with power, even though you know how powerless you actually feel. They will also perceive you as someone who has lots of money. Maybe you do, maybe you don't. Either way, your tenant is going to think you are rich.

We took an application from a young man who thought anyone who owned a house with a *one*-car garage was rich. So if you have tenants who define rich by having a one-car garage, they're going to think you are a multi-millionaire with your two-car garage, even though they're the ones driving a new car and you're still tooling around in a ten year old truck.

No matter how rich or poor you are, the less the tenant knows of your financial situation the better. Avoid appearing richer than you already do. When you show properties dress for the neighborhood. In a lower income area, you don't need to wear a business suit, jeans and t-shirt are fine. In a middle-class neighborhood, wear comfortable slacks and a nice clean shirt. Only wear business apparel if you're renting a mansion.

The same goes with a car. For showing properties in lower income neighborhoods drive your beater and leave the Mercedes at home in your three-car garage.

Even though you don't want to appear rich, neither do you want to let on how many bills you have and their requests for repairs are sending you to the poor house. That may be exactly what your tenants want, so don't give them the satisfaction.

Quiet Enjoyment

Basically quiet enjoyment means the tenant gets to live in the property without you coming over and bugging them all the time. You need to respect the tenant's privacy and follow the laws in your state regarding inspection of the home. Quiet enjoyment means you need to detach from the rental property.

The house you are renting may have some emotional meaning to you. Maybe you lived there for years, or maybe it was your mother's home, or maybe it was a house that you fixed up all by yourself and you take pride in all your hard work. Or maybe it is simply an investment property to you, and represents your kid's college education or early retirement. All of these are reasons to be involved with what is going on at your rental.

In spite of your concern, interest and investment in your property, you must contain yourself and avoid mingling in the tenant's lives. You don't need to check up on them all the time. If you have a burning desire to know what is going on at your property, arrange to go by every month and pick up the rent checks. But it is better to just let it go. Drive by every once in awhile and make sure the house is still standing, the lawn is being mowed and seven cars aren't parked in the driveway. You can even drive by late at night to make sure loud and crazy parties aren't going on. However, as long as your tenants are not in violation of the lease, leave them alone.

Although our personal preference is not to rent to smokers, we do anyway. Not only is smoking a nasty habit a fire hazard but the cigarette smell seeps in the walls and carpets and is very difficult to get completely out of the house. Although discriminating against smokers is legal, what is the point? How can you be certain if people are smoking in your house or not? If you put in the lease that smoking is not allowed in your house, and you come over to collect the rent and smell the distinctive aroma of cancer sticks, are you really going to evict and start the entire process over again?

Instead of worrying about whether or not someone is smoking in your house or whether or not they are taking care of your roses, you need to give yourself a thorough reality check.

A lot of tenants are "hard" on a property, but at the same time they're not destroying it. Let it go. How your tenants take care of your property is not a reflection on you.

It is especially important as a landlord to not create drama and to stay out of your tenant's drama. If you find yourself worrying about the house because the tenant isn't taking care of the lawn as nicely as you would, you are starting to create drama. In doing so, you may find yourself complaining to anyone who will listen about your lousy tenants. You may even call the tenant to tell them they need to take better care of the yard, or you may start going over to the rental and doing the yard work yourself. These are non-productive behaviors and may eventually cost you a tenant.

On the same token, some of your tenants may call you for various reasons, usually for a repair or to tell you they will be late with the rent. Along with the phone call will come a story. Perhaps the tenant lost a job, has a car in need of repair, a sick baby, getting a divorce...you name it. You may actually end up knowing more about your tenants' lives than their own family. Whatever is going in your tenants lives is not your problem. You can be sympathetic with your tenants' problems but it is not your job to solve them and you do not need to be drawn into the drama of your tenants' situation.

Both creating drama yourself and being drawn into other people's drama will take an emotional toll. There is enough drama in property management, you don't need to add any of your own.

Chapter Nine

Repairs

Those of you who have the time and are able to do most of the repairs on your rental property, can save a lot of money. On the other hand, those of you who don't know the first thing about repairs will have to hire service providers to take care of the problems. The good news is all those repair costs are tax deductable.

Handymen

When you are unable to do the work yourself, you will need to find a good handyman. A good handyman is hard to find. The reason being good ones are always busy and you may have to be put on a waiting list. The handyman who is readily available may not do the quality of work you would expect for what he charges.

There are basically two types of handymen. One who works through a service company and the type who works on his own.

A handyman service can usually be found in business section of the telephone book, the service guide in the newspaper and online. These services will have someone come out and give you an estimate, after which, you can schedule the job to be completed. It will often take a handyman service three to seven days to schedule an estimate and you will probably have to wait a week or more for them to do the work. Another disadvantage is these handyman services charge premium prices. However, they do hire experienced contractors to do the job and they will usually guarantee the work. The service company can also bill you for the work and will sometimes take Master Card or Visa.

The other type of handyman is much more casual, they are not really business people and will go from job to job. They rarely have anyone to answer the phone, and will pick it up themselves or you will have to leave a message. If they are on a job, they may not call you back for a week. If these handymen are good at what they do, you need to act fast, because they're in high demand and you don't want to be at the bottom of their list. A lot of times these handymen don't like to come out and do estimates, when they come out, they expect to do the job. Usually, they'll give you an idea of what it will cost over the phone. Honest ones will keep to that price or once on the job tell you right away it will be more. Beware of the scammers out who will tell you one price and have it doubled by the time the work is through.

These handymen can do a variety of repairs, are often unlicensed, and expect to be paid cash at the end of the job. The advantage to using them, is they are often a lot cheaper than a licensed service provider. They will usually advertise in the service section of the classifieds. Sometimes you can find them the in a business section of the telephone, but the best way to find a decent handyman is through word of mouth. Ask everyone you know who they recommend for jobs around the house.

Since so many handymen tend to be unreliable, dishonest and/or don't know what they're doing, you should hire them to do a small job for you first. In fact, you can test out your new handyman on a few repairs in your own house you've been putting off.

When the handyman is at your home, watch him work, and ask him questions about what he can and cannot do. Here are some questions you might want to ask:

- Does he charge by the hour or the job?
- Are the materials included in the cost or are they extra?
- What experience does he have?
- Does he have any licenses?
- Will he work weekends?
- Does he guarantee his work?
-

When the handyman leaves you can ask yourself these questions:

- Did he arrive on time?
- Was he professional?
- Were you comfortable around him?
- Did he charge more than he initially said?
- Did he do the job correctly and in a timely manner?

You should try and find at least two handymen to put on your call list.

Other Service Providers

There are a few areas where you absolutely want to get the job done promptly and correctly, especially heating, plumbing and electrical. You may not be able to wait for a handyman. By law, you need to provide your tenant with running water and heat. You do not need to provide air conditioning and other amenities. However, whatever appliances you supplied with the rental, you will have to replace or repair.

When it comes to large repairs for such as electrical, plumbing and heat/air, many states require the service provider to have a license. Find out what the requirements are for your state. For instance in California, any work over $500 will have to be done by a licensed contractor. Although more expensive than a handyman, the work is often guaranteed to be done correctly. Repairs that are done incorrectly are very aggravating and adds even more cost to you.

To find one of these licensed professionals, simply go online or to the business section of the telephone book. Unfortunately, just because a contractor is has a big ad in the phone book, extensive advertising online, or has a well-known franchise doesn't mean they are honest.

Many small and large service providers seem to have a business model of overcharging by thousands of dollars. They know they will only get a fraction of the jobs, but the jobs they get will be money makers.

One time we had a tenant complaining that the furnace motor was coming on but she couldn't get any heat. We were new to the area and didn't have any service people lined up, so we called an ad out of the business section of the phone book. The guy came out and looked at it, and told us we needed a whole new heating unit, the cost would be between three and four thousand dollars. Oh my!

Then we remembered what happened at another rental in another state. The air conditioner hadn't been working and the big name service provider wanted to put in another unit costing about $5000. Fortunately, we had the presence of mind to call another air conditioning company. They came out and fixed the air conditioner for around $150. So we told the heater repair guy, "thanks but no thanks," and called another service contractor. Sure enough, this guy was able to come out and repair the problem for under a hundred dollars.

In another instance, we had a tenant call about a hot water heating problem and we were unable to reach the regular plumber we normally use. The tenant was in a panic and called a national plumbing franchise to come out and look at the problem. The repair person told us we needed a whole new water heater and also some piping repairs around the area which would require taking out a wall. The cost would be just under $3000. Three thousand dollars for a new hot water heater!? The next day, we had our regular plumber come out and he fixed the leak on the spot for around $200, and told us that although it wasn't the best quality water heater we didn't need a new one as it was only a couple of years old. Whew!

This types of scamming by so-called legitimate contractors happens all the time! So be skeptical of any estimate that seems too costly. If necessary, get a couple of opinions. We have noticed the honest ones charge more per hour than the scammers – the scam operators are trying to pull you in on their lower price so they can lower the boom once they've looked at the job.

Especially beware of service providers sent out by your home warranty company. Many sellers will provide the purchaser of the property a one year home warranty to cover some repairs that might happen. The seller does this to protect themselves from the buyer coming back and trying to sue them for heating and other systems that might break down the minute the new owner takes over. These home warranties will send out a service provider on their list, and the owner is charged a fee -- between $50 to $100 -- each time someone comes out. The cost of the repair beyond that price is paid for by the home warranty company.

The trick service providers sent out by home warranty companies pull is to claim, "improper install." The home warranty company will not pay for this, and the service provider can jack up the bill by several hundred to several thousand dollars. If this happens to you, tell the service provider your policy is to always get a second opinion. You can also add that if another provider comes out and finds it was installed correctly, you will report this to the home warranty company. The home warranty company won't do anything, but it might give the service provider a little scare.

When you come across a handyman or service provider who is honest and does good work, put them on your "First to Call" list. Create good karma by being pleasant with whoever answers the phone and pay your service provider promptly. Refer a good handyman as much business as you can.

On the other hand, when a service provider tries to gouge you with unnecessary repairs or does shoddy work, put them on a "Do Not Use" list. You can go online to various websites and warn others about their poor business practices. Believe it or not, if enough people take this advice, a lot of service providers would shape-up or go out of business.

Plumbing

Plumbing issues should be taken care of as quickly as possible. Prolonged leaks will destroy the nearby wood and necessitate even more repair costs. When wood gets soaked it can start to rot and may even continue rotting after it is dry, thus the term dry rot. If you are paying the water bill, even a tiny leak can add several dollars to each month's bill. In the long run it is cheaper to get the leaks repaired ASAP.

One of the most aggravating problems is the running toilet. You can put in a whole new plunger system, but if the toilet flap is not sealing properly, you will still have a problem. Sometimes the chain is too tight leaving the flap open just a bit; you can simply put the chain on another link and see if that solves it. Run your finger around the rim covered by the flap and make sure it is smooth and not chipped or has water deposit buildup.

Another common toilet problem, is the wax seal beneath the toilet connecting it to the sewer fails. This is a matter of removing the toilet and replacing the seal. Sometimes a longer sewer pipe is needed if for some reason the distance between the top of the pipe and the floor has changed, like settling, or someone tiled the floor over old linoleum.

Sometimes pipes will break. This usually happens if they froze or if they were installed incorrectly. A water burst will probably necessitate an insurance claim because water will be everywhere in the house soaking carpets and wood. You will need to get a water damage restoration expert to dry it out your property. Cleaning it up yourself and letting it dry on its own may save you some initial money; but you will not be able to get all the water out and mold and mildew will start growing. The rental will take on a permanent "stale" smell and you may experience some dry rot problems.

Besides leaks, stoppages are another of the most common problems tenants call about. The good news about stoppages is if you can show the tenant had clear drainage when they took the place, then they most likely created the stoppage and will have to pay for it. The exception to this would be roots in the sewer line or some other collapse of the pipe beyond the tenant's control.

Handling stoppages caused by the tenant can be tricky. One way to handle plumbing stoppages that is the fault of the tenant is to go ahead and pay for the repair yourself. Then take those repair costs out of the deposit. If you insist on payment from the tenant at the time of occurrence, they might not tell you about other plumbing issues and leave you with an expensive wet mess.

Hot Water Heater

Hot water heaters generally last for ten or more years. They can often be repaired fairly inexpensively unless the glass is broken or it is starting to rust. The hot water heater should be off the ground by an inch or so and should not sit directly on brick or concrete as the moist heat will cause them to deteriorate. Hot water heaters need to "breathe" and if they are in a closet, it should be vented.

Electrical

Usually electrical problems are old switches and outlets that need to be replaced. The other problem is older houses still on fuses or using old technology circuit breakers. If the tenant is using too much electric on the same fuse or circuit, it will keep popping. Older homes are not equipped for the number of appliances in use today. You can explain this to the tenant, and if they don't like it they can move to a more modern place. In the long run, however, it is beneficial to upgrade the electrical from fuses to circuit breakers. Many insurance carriers will not insure if they know the property is still on fuses because of the high fire hazard.

Heat/Air Conditioning

Air conditioners and heaters appliances need to be serviced quite frequently especially as they get older. The repairs generally run around $100 - $300 depending on the year, make and model. In your lease make it the tenant's responsibility to change the air filter in a timely manner.

Evaporative cooler filters are the landlord's responsibility. The filters should be changed every spring as they are a breeding ground for bacteria.

Garbage Disposals/Dishwashers

Many tenants don't know how to use garbage disposals. They will put anything down there that will fit through the drain including metal. You may decide to be nice and allow one garbage disposal repair. Any subsequent calls or if the service guy says it needs to be replaced, simply have him remove it.

Built in dishwashers will have to be repaired in nicer homes, but in lower end rentals, when it is time for replacement you can have it removed. We have found in lower income homes, tenants actually prefer the extra cabinet space rather than a dishwasher.

Refrigerators and Other Appliances

Refrigerators are always costly to repair, and it is generally cheaper to put in a new one rather than repairing the old one. Never buy a tenant a new refrigerator. If you want a new refrigerator, buy one for yourself and give the tenant your old one. The best way to handle refrigerators is not at all. Let the tenant supply their own refrigerator. If there is a old refrigerator already at the rental, possibly left behind by the previous tenant, "give" the tenant the refrigerator and any repairs or replacements is their problem. Be sure you put in the lease, that the refrigerator is supplied by the tenant.

The only other appliance you need to supply is the stove and oven. These are usually fairly inexpensive to repair or replace if necessary.

Broken Windows, Doors

If you gave the tenant a property without any broken windows, then the tenant is responsible for repairing any breakage. They may claim someone tried to break in their house, in which case you will have to do the repair providing the tenant has a police report. If the tenant cannot produce a police report, then the tenant is liable for the repair.

Sometimes cheaper housing will have hollow wood doors (interior doors) as an exterior door. These are easy to kick in and do not weather very well. Eventually you will want to change these over to windowless metal doors. All exterior doors should have working locks and deadbolts, with an additional security hasp. When an old tenant moves out, you need to have all the exterior doors rekeyed. This is for the security of the new tenant as you have no idea how many keys the previous tenant passed out and to whom. When you have one key that opens all the locks to one rental, it makes it easier to keep track of keys especially if you own several properties.

Leaking Roof

A leaking roof needs to be repaired as soon as possible. Although you may want to delay putting on a new roof for as long as possible, you must keep the roof in good repair. A damaged, leaking roof can create problems and cost you money in the long run. When one side of the roof faces south or receives more sun and weather exposure, sometimes only that portion of the roof will need to be replaced. Keep the shingle colors the same and no one will notice the difference.

Mold

From time to time the local news will run a scary story about black mold. You will know when this happens, because suddenly your tenants will be calling about getting leaks repaired and feeling sick. You do want to get mold issues taken care of as quickly as possible.

The first thing to do is eliminate the source of leaking otherwise all your other efforts will be in vain. The leaks can be anywhere in or around your home from under the house, within the walls or in the attic. Once the leaks have been removed you can take the necessary steps to eliminate the mold, which may include replacement of wood and scrubbing the area with liquid bleach.

One time we managed a property and found very good tenants who had lived happily in a rental for about a year. No problems. They paid their rent on time and we enjoyed visiting with them when coming over to collect. However, one day a pipe burst and much of the carpet in the house was soaked. The homeowner's insurance paid for the clean-up, but the carpet was ruined. We received permission from the owner and ordered the new carpeting.

When the carpet installers pulled out the old carpet and padding, they told the tenant there was black mold growing on the floor beneath the carpet. There was some dark damp residue in one of the bedrooms, and different areas of the concrete floor had huge black spots. First of all, these guys were carpet layers and not experts in black mold. Second, the minute the workers were convinced there was a black mold issue in the house, they should have stopped installing the carpet.

We received a message from the tenants there was a problem with the house. It sounded like a dire emergency, but they didn't say what the problem was. When we received the message we tried calling them and they did not answer. We decided to go over to the property and see what was going on. By the time we arrived, the installers were nearly finished with the job.

"Black mold," the tenants said in a panic. "The house is filled with black mold, we've been getting sick, and headaches." Funny, they hadn't complained about being sick and headaches before. They showed us the carpet padding with the black blotches and the part in the bedroom where the dampness was.

We knew the tenants were over-reacting. Nevertheless, based on an assessment by carpet layers, they decided to move. We complained to the carpet company saying their installers had no business telling the tenants there was a black mold issue when they were carpet installers and not black mold experts. We told the carpet store owner, when the installers saw there was a problem, they should have stopped rather than continuing with the installation. If there really was a black mold issue, the carpet would have to be taken out. That being the case, and because the installers cost us a tenant, we would not paying for the carpet. If they desired, the company could have someone come back out and take their carpeting.

The carpet store owner consulted with his attorney who sent us a threatening collections letter. We responded to the attorney's letter putting in writing the same issues we had discussed with the owner. Nothing further happened. The company never pressed for payment and they never came and took out the carpet.

In the meantime, we now had an empty unit. The former happy tenants -- now disgruntled -- were telling everyone in the neighborhood the house was contaminated. We had several potential new tenants decide not to move in after talking to the former tenants.

We told the owner of the problem who decided to pay for a professional black mold testing, which was quite costly. That way, if there truly was an issue we could resolve it. Guess what, the test came back proving NO black mold was in the house, not even in the room with the damp spot. With this test in hand, we were able to rent the property.

If a tenant insists that mold is in the house and making them sick, let them move. In fact, encourage them to move. Once tenants have it in their head the house is contaminated, they could cause a legal headache for you. In addition, if the house truly is contaminated they shouldn't be living there and if it's not contaminated they tend not to believe you without a black mold test.

Pests

If you have a multi-unit you will have to take care of pest problems and may want to pay for a monthly service. In single family homes, you can offer one spray, or if you prefer spray before the new tenants move in. After that, they are responsible for their own pest removal. Make sure this is indicated in your lease.

Mice and rats are a special problem and often indicates there is water leaking somewhere in the house, so find the water source. In addition, seal pipes and cracks making it more difficult for vermin to get in. Once that is taken care of, have the exterminator come out. Sometimes these critters get in the pipes and between the walls. If they die somewhere within the confines of the house, it will stink for awhile. Unless you can find the dead animal, the stench will remain for awhile but eventually go away on its own. You need to warn the tenant of this possibility. If the problem continues, the tenant is likely luring them in by keeping people and/or pet food out and not keeping a clean house.

Rent Reduction

Sometimes tenants will be willing to do some of the repair work themselves and in return expect some money off the rent. Although a tempting offer -- especially when it seems impossible to find anyone available to come out and do the work – be careful when allowing tenants to make repairs as they may try to take advantage. If you are going to pay the tenant for repairs, be sure and require the following:

- Your approval to do the work
- Cap how much you will pay
- You must see the final product
- They must give you an receipts.

A trick tenants like to play is complaining about certain repairs and do them in exchange for rent, which is fine, but it is possible there wasn't anything wrong to begin with or they never actually did any repairs. We rented to a retired contractor who was always finding problems with the property. These were minor repairs like an electrical switch was needed or the sprinkler system line was broken. He was more than willing to fix the problems and bill us, which we deducted from the rent. He charged a reasonable price, he did good work...except, every single month some kind of repair was needed. Odder still, the house was less than a year old. We stopped approving the repairs and the tenant found another place to live.

You want to get legitimate repairs taken care of as soon as possible, but you must discern if a tenant is simply looking for re-duced rent. Most tenants are good about telling you about repairs that need to be done and rarely bother you with trivial issues.

Chapter Ten

Rent is the Priority

Before becoming landlords, one of our greatest concerns was rent collection. We had spoken to people who managed some of their own rental properties and they had a terrible time collecting rent. We were told they would go by to pick up the rent, and the tenant would apologize and say come back after pay-day next week, only to be told the same story again. One man told us, he had a tenant who had been living in one of his houses for over six months and had never paid a dime of rent. We know of other landlords who have let tenants stay for over a year without paying rent. Yikes!

Nip late and non-payment of the rent in the bud.

Our lease states rent is due on the first of the month, and when rent is considered late. Technically, if your lease does not say when rent is due, then the tenant has the entire month to pay the rent. We usually give a three to five day grace period for tenants to pay without charging a late fee. Since we do not allow tenants to mail in rent checks, we know immediately if they are late or not.

On the *first* day after the grace period, we post a pay or quit notice. On the notice we include the late and posting fees. Beware, not all states allow you to include these fees on the pay or quit notice. Some states like California will only permit you to put the rent amount as specified in the lease and including any other fees will invalidate the notice.

If the tenants call to tell us they will pay in full by the fifteenth, we tell them that's okay and remind them how much the late charges will be. We also make it clear, if the money is not there as promised on the fifteenth; on the sixteenth, we will proceed with the eviction.

Other times we will receive a phone call asking to accept a partial payment on Friday, and the tenant will pay balance sometime in the middle of the month. We also agree to this, with the warning if we do not receive the partial payment as agreed, the following Monday we will start the unlawful detainer action. Once a partial payment is received, the pay or quit notice becomes null and void. Immediately upon receipt of a partial payment, we post a pay or quit notice, but inform the tenant we will not proceed until after the date they promised to pay the balance of the rent.

We really push to get the rent paid early in the month, but will work with tenants as long as they are honest with us. If a tenant finally gets the rent paid at the end of the month, it is a certainty they will not be able to pay the rent at the beginning of the next month.

If a tenant does not call, and does not pay within the specified time period, we start the eviction. We do not call and beg them to pay the rent, we do not keep going by to see if they're home and they'll give us some money. We just start the unlawful detainer proceedings.

Does this sound mean and tough to you? Does it sound like we're rotten people because we insist that the rent is paid promptly each month? Notice we will work with tenants who are honest with us and will do as they say. We have worked with tenants to get caught up with their rent over a period of months.

Most tenants will pay the rent if they have the money. What happens is that hardships occur and fixing the car or paying the doctor bill becomes more important than paying the rent. Unfortunately, for many, many tenants in all socio-economic groups rent is not a priority.

Let's talk priorities. Shouldn't family and children be the number one priority?

Absolutely.

Remember paying the rent is a fundamental key in taking care of children, and is almost as important as feeding them. We always paid our rent/mortgages, and when we were new to the rental game, the negative impact non-payment of rent on children was foreign to us. Managing properties over time, we saw the effects not paying the rent has on kids.

When parents don't pay the rent, they are subject to evictions and move a lot, creating an unstable environment for the children. Usually children are vibrant and curious. They may be shy, but are rarely withdrawn. Every time we have rented to a family where the children were sullen and withdrawn, we eventually had to do an eviction. The children from non-renting paying parents know never to get close to anyone because they are moving soon. They know they are moving in a shameful way.

On the positive side, parents who make paying the rent a priority, is a value that seeps through to the children -- even though the parent may never say a word to the child about paying the rent on time. Parents who pay their rent on time help create children to become better adults.

My partner and I were discussing the problem of tenants whose rent was not a priority. He suggested children learned to pay or not pay rent from their parents. "How?" I asked, and told him that my grown children paid their rent and I had never in my life told them to make rent a priority. Neither had my parents stressed to me about paying the rent first. But I always paid my rent, even when I was a young single mom waiting tables and over half my income went toward housing. Every day after work, I literally counted the dollars and change I made in tips to get the rent paid – and it was always on time – never a late fee. My partner said, "You didn't have to tell her, she saw it, and that's how children learn." Wow.

Rent should be a priority because housing is a basic human need. Tenants need to learn they are in a contract and they must honor what they signed. They need to learn how to budget, and decide that food and shelter are more important than fancy clothes and a new car. A lot of tenants cop an attitude that the landlord owes them a place to live. These tenants seem to think of their landlord as a parent who must supply them a home. When rent is not a priority, it becomes your job as a landlord to help your tenants grow up.

Never, ever feel guilty for conducting an eviction. You are actually doing the community a service by getting the bums out of the neighborhood. You are teaching non-paying tenants an important lesson in life that they never got at home.

If more landlords took a hard-nosed attitude about paying rent on time, the quality of tenants would go up everywhere and for everyone. When landlords refuse to put up with late rent, they will get their rent paid in full. Sometimes a landlord is the first person in someone's life who actually holds them to their word and makes them accountable. Being a parent to your tenant was probably not a job you thought you would be doing. Since tenants are not your kids, stay out of their drama and start the eviction process promptly.

Our policy is that once we have paid court costs for the eviction, we do not stop the process unless the tenant agrees to pay all our costs to date and catch up on the rent including late and posting fees. We had a attorney who suggested also collecting next month's rent since they established themselves to be late payers. Not a bad idea.

Chapter Eleven

Problem Tenants

Dealing with tenants is one of the main reasons people are reluctant or even afraid to invest in residential real estate. The key to success is to find good tenants and to keep them as long as possible, which is one reason sometimes tenants are in a property for many years and paying rent far below market. They are probably good tenants and the landlord doesn't want to lose them.

Problem tenants show up in a variety of forms. You may find certain tenants will "test" you and your resolve. These tenants are like children discovering your boundaries, what you will put up with and what you won't. Testing tactics will come in a variety of guises and excuses. To be a successful landlord, you must be firm with your requirements and not hesitate to do whatever is necessary -- including evict -- if your tenants become too much of a problem.

A common strategy a tenant will use to test the landlord is to be late with the rent. No matter what the excuse or lack thereof, the tenant may be checking to see how quickly you follow-up, how badly you want the rent, and whether or not you will enforce late fees.

Speaking of late fees, if collecting them promptly from the tenant seems daunting, intimidating, or impossible, remember you can deduct these fees from the deposit. Keep an accurate account of dates rents are paid and of any unpaid fees.

Whiners/Complainers

Usually when tenants move into a rental, they discover problems you were unaware of. Of course you want to take care of these issues as soon as possible. You want to make your tenant feel secure that legitimate repairs will be dealt with promptly. However, if the tenants keep finding more and more problems – even if legitimate – after they have been living on the premises for more than a month, you have a problem.

We managed a duplex, and rented to a family who seemed very good. They paid their rent promptly on the first of every month. Yet every single month there was a repair problem. What was even more disconcerting was that all of their requests were legitimate. They ranged from plumbing, electrical, heat and air. What we didn't understand was why one unit was having all these problems and yet the other side had none.

When the air conditioning wasn't working during the hottest part of the summer, the tenants left the unit and stayed at a motel until the air conditioning was fixed asserting we should pay for their motel stay. According to the lease they signed we were not liable for their decision to rent a motel. Next the tenants started complaining that their utility bill was too high. The tenants insisted was something very wrong with the unit and until we found out what the problem was wanted us to *pay a portion of their electric bill.*

This was the final straw. We told them, they needed to get the utility company out there to determine if there was any other reason – beyond the fact they ran their air conditioner 24/7 at 68° -- causing the high utility bills. Naturally, the utility company found nothing. To top it off, several handymen had come out in response to their problems and found things as simple as needing to change the furnace filter – according to the lease, their job. We kept note of the fees and eventually took the service charge out of the tenant's deposit.

In the meantime, we had repaired everything: the heat, the air, the ducts, the bathtub leaking, the leaking under the bathroom sink, broken lock, the sewer drain, exterminated rats and all should be fine now right? Wrong.

The next month, we received an emergency call that some-one had broken into their unit and kicked in the back door. They had a police report to show there was really a burglary. A burglary? Or had they locked themselves out and kicked in the door, calling it a burglary to save paying the lockout fee?

We called a handyman and he gave a quote for the repair at over $500. He claimed the repair required a whole new door. When we looked at it, the metal door was fine, only the door jamb needed to be repaired. In the meantime, the tenants had bolted some hasps into the walls and kept the door secure with a 2x4 barring the door and keeping it closed.

Because the door was secured and because they were complainers, we let them wait on this particular repair. We had another handyman who could take care of the problem much, much cheaper, but he was busy, and they would have to wait.

At this point, they had been living at the property for a year. Time to raise the rent. We raised it ten percent. The tenant called us all happy, "Oh, you're going to remodel?"

Huh? We told her, "No, we're raising the rent and we're not remodeling, and if you don't like it you can move."

She was shocked that we had the audacity to raise her rent and not remodel. We repeated, "If you don't like it, move."

They didn't catch our hint that maybe we wanted them out. The tenants continued to live at the duplex for many years, but after the rent increase, stopped complaining.

Tenant Repairs/Improvements

Tenants will often want to do work on the property in exchange for reduced rent. We often agree to have tenants make repairs and take the cost off their next months rent. We ascertain the repairs are legitimate and the tenant usually charges significantly less than the cost of a handyman.

However, your tenant may also want rent reduction for painting or beautification of your property. It is always nice when the tenant wants to do improvements; it is nicer when they don't expect anything in return...and those type of tenants are out there. By the way, we allow tenants to paint interior walls and color they like – even black if they so desire – with the proviso they return the wall to the original color (white or off-white) when they move. Most tenants are happy to be able to decorate how they want and tend to stay longer.

However, be reluctant to pay tenants who expect re-imbursement for their non-repair related work. In some ways rent reduction especially for supplies seems fair, but sometimes these improvements are ploys to obtain reduced rent. If that is their ultimate aim, they'll want to do something about every month, and when you approved it the first time, you set yourself up for more rent reductions in the future. When a tenant wants to be paid for "fixing up" your property, you can say:

"Most of my other tenants will do this work on their own dime, and it's not fair to them to give you a break."

You can also remind your tenant that per the lease they accepted the property as-is. Let the tenants decide whether or not they really want to do home improvements using their own money. If all they truly want is reduced rent, they will likely find a landlord who can be railroaded a little easier and move.

Another trick tenants like to play is the "I was in-convenienced and so you owe me" game. This happens when the heat doesn't work and it takes three days for the repairman to get out. In the meantime, you can supply the tenants with some space heaters. When the air conditioning is broken, they can use fans or a small room air conditioner. If you agree to reimburse tenants because they had to stay at a motel, rather than paying for the cost of the motel, calculate how much rent they pay per day times the number of days they were gone and deduct that amount from the rent. Your lease should have a clause about delayed repairs and they cannot hold you liable for their decision to live elsewhere until the repairs are made.

Many states have a law that allows a tenant to have the repair done themselves and take it off the rent, as long as they give the landlord a copy of the receipt. In spite of the law and the wording in your lease, tenants often threaten not to pay rent until repairs are done. Complete the repairs and collect the rent along with late fees, then seriously consider the pros and cons of giving tenants who blackmail you repairs for rent a thirty-day notice to move.

Trash/Cars/Destruction

It seems most tenants keep their homes reasonably clean and do not destroy it. A few, however, are very hard on the home. We had a tenant who never cleaned and simply didn't take care of things. She did pay her rent on time. Every year we raised the rent and she continued to pay on time. Eventually the tenant was paying above market rent. Don't worry about dirt, you can clean, paint and exterminate when the tenant leaves.

Many times you will see tenants parking cars everywhere, including on the lawn in the front and back yard. However, if the neighbors and city don't complain, and they are paying their rent, don't worry about it. Raise their rent every year. If you receive complaints about their cars or garbage, enforce the lease and make them get rid of it. Deduct any lawn repairs from the deposit.

When a tenant is hard on a home and causing destruction, versus normal wear and tear, you can charge them for the damages. Keep track of everything they owe. Taking before and after pictures will help bolster your case if you take them to court.

Liars/Manipulators

The most common lie tenants tell will be about the rent and why they will be late. They will make promises to have the rent in on their next payday, and when payday comes they only give you half the rent. Then the tenant will make another promise to get caught up next week. Allowing this behavior to continue means eventually your tenants will be a month or more behind on their rent. You must be diligent on your pay or quit notices and not accept partial payments.

There is a difference between tenants who lie about paying the rent, and tenants who are late payers. You will find that due to paycheck and budget constraints many of your tenants are chronic late payers. However, the tenant will call you and tell you the situation and pay as promised along with the late fee. Liars, however, will promise, promise, promise and not deliver. Every time you come for the rent, you will hear a new excuse, usually something about not getting paid.

Tenants will also lie about repairs they have completed. Or they may say they got something repaired and make up how much it cost. You need to see both the completed repair and the receipt. One of our tenants told us that she had gotten someone to repair her faulty door. We thought the price she paid was reasonable and she said she had a receipt. When we came to pick up the receipt, the door had not been repaired. She was simply trying to get some money out of us.

Beware of tenants who want to be your friend.

Manipulators cozy up to you. They will compliment you and act like they are your best friend. They want something, but it may not necessarily be reduced rent. They may be hiding something in the home or doing something illegal.

Drugs

You do not want is tenants dealing drugs or other illegal substances on your property. You especially don't want them to start a meth lab in your kitchen. If you have a renter involved in illegal activities, they will probably behave like an ideal tenant. They will pay their rent on time and never complain -- they don't want you to come sniffing around their business. That being the case, you may not realize they have an illegitimate home-based business.

One thing drug dealers are looking for is easy access for a quick in and out. They prefer absentee owners or property managers who are indifferent to their actions. They also want privacy, and if your property doesn't have a security fence or hedge blocking the front door, they may put one in with our without your permission.

One of the most obvious signs of drug dealing is a lot of people coming in and out. Another sign is if they don't let you inside when you collect the rent. You should not enter the premises without the tenant's permission except in emergency situations. Most states have laws that force the landlord to give the tenant twenty-four or more hours notice to inspect the property. By that time, the tenants will have hidden the evidence. If you suspect drugs, you can conduct routine inspections of the premises every month. The tenant won't like that and will move.

Retaliators

There are two major ways tenants will retaliate against the landlord. The first is to trash the property. Of course, many tenants just leave the property trashed without any malice toward the landlord whatsoever. However, the retaliator will come up with creative ways to make your life miserable and cost you money. The retaliator may cut electrical lines and put things like cement in the toilet. You need to keep track of the cost of the repairs for lawsuit and collection purposes.

Another devious trick tenant will place is call the city housing inspector and claim the house is uninhabitable. The inspector will *always* find a series of petty little things and issue a correction order. You will have several months to make the repairs and can usually ask for an extension. But you will have to do the work and the city must approve it. Keep track of how much the tenant's phone call to the city cost you and deduct it from their deposit.

The Nineteen Year Old Hellion

One time a mother with two children applied to rent one of our units. Although she looked nearly 30, according to the application she was only 19 years old. Being 19, Christina had no previous rental history and her sole source of income was from welfare. We politely took the application and continued looking for a better tenant. When Christina followed up on the application, we explained her income was too low and therefore she didn't qualify.

For some reason, Christina was bound and determined to rent the place. A few days later her father put in an application, he had a guaranteed income from a disability but he also had a payee who would ensure the rent was paid. We were familiar with the non-profit agency that would be paying his bills, so we rented to him. Realizing his daughter would also be living at the place, we put the lease exclusively in the father's name, but listed Christina and grandchildren as occupants.

For nearly a year, all was well. During this time we moved out of the state. Then the inevitable happened, one month the rent didn't come. First, we called the agency to hear our tenant was no longer in the system, and then we called the tenant. Christina answered the phone and matter-of-factly told us her father was in prison but she would continue to stay and pay the rent. And she did. For six months she was a good little payer, and we almost thought our original instincts about her were wrong.

But then one month Christina called complaining about the place and gave us a litany of everything wrong with it and she refused to pay rent until all the repairs were made. Well, this was the first we knew about any problems, but the repairs were legitimate so we went ahead and authorized repairs which included new flooring in the bathroom. When the repairs were made, she still refused to pay the rent. We started the eviction process.

We knew the eviction would be a piece of cake since the father was on the lease and being in prison, he would not be able to appear in court. Nevertheless, Christina went to legal aid and answered the complaint. The courts allowed her answer to be submitted because she resided in the rental before the unlawful detainer action was filed.

The good news was she left the unit anyway possibly because she knew of our policy to inform social services of any pending eviction when there are children involved. Christina left a message on our phone saying she was out, and I called back asking about the key. Well, she gave me an earful that what we were doing was wrong blah, blah, blah and she wouldn't be returning the key until the court day. What Christina didn't understand was she had already vacated the place thus negating any need for a court appearance. We kept the message where she stated she was gone, cancelled the court proceeding, and hired a locksmith to rekey the place.

The locksmith told us Christina had left the water running, destroyed the new carpet with cigarette burns, and punched holes in the walls. At this point, we had started managing the unit long distance, but we knew the drill. We put the property on the market through Craig's list and explained about the mess and repairs. In payment for repairs, the new tenant could have off the first month's rent. In the meantime, Christina called the city and had the unit red-tagged meaning no one could move in until the repairs were made and the city gave their approval. Worse, Christina had her friends start dumping trash in the backyard of the property. Every night a fresh load was dumped in the yard. We called the police, as usual, they took the report and did nothing.

In spite of all Christina's mischief we found a new tenant who was willing to haul away the trash, perform the repairs, paint and clean up the place for reduced rent. She worked with the city to remove the red tag, paid the rent, and never complained – exactly the type of tenant what we were looking for. Of course, Christina was upset that we were able to rent the place so easily and called leaving me a horrible message about what a bad person I was. We could never figure out why she had so much anger directed specifically at me – maybe mother issues.

At any rate, after deducting Christina's deposit we calculated the damages and money still owed and sent a bill to the collection agency for over $3000. When Christina received her first collection call, she left me another hateful message this with an underlying threat -- another reason you don't want tenants to know where you live.

Soap Operas

If you enjoy soap operas and like hearing about the drama of other people's lives, you will love being a landlord. In some cases, you will know more of what goes on in a tenant's life then their own family. You will hear their stories especially if you come around and collect the rent in person. Otherwise, you'll gather up snippets on emails and phone messages.

We had a tenant crying to us because her mother was in the hospital possibly dying. She was too young to be losing her mother and it was very sad.

The story didn't stop there, however. Her mother was a drug addict, and the doctors were trying to save her, yet didn't give the mother much hope. The mother had cirrhosis of the liver and was in intense physical pain. Because of the nature of her addiction, the doctors weren't giving her the "strong stuff," so the woman was experiencing intense suffering. The mother's friends were sneaking vodka and other pain relievers to help alleviate the pain. In addition, the tenant's mother was in a hospital out of town so the tenant wasn't able to go see her because she didn't have money for gas. While telling me this horrible story she was crying and counting out the rent.

Listen, take the rent, and give your sincere condolences along with the rent receipt.

In another case, the tenant started crying because she and her husband were breaking up. She plopped a big fat tear on the rent check. We listened to her story, asked what her plans were about staying or moving, took the check and gave our condolences.

Another tenant had her pay garnished by the IRS. The situation seemed terribly unfair, because the garnishment came from her ex-husband's business and the IRS couldn't find him. Because she had been a partner to his business plans, she was liable to the IRS. She still had to pay rent.

The tenant's problems are not your problems, you have enough of your own to worry about theirs. Listen, sympathize take the rent and go. Sound cruel? Property management hardens you. It's okay if you cry right along with the tenant, but you still must resist the urge to reduce their rent. If you have too much of a soft spot, hire yourself a good property management firm to deal with the tenant's drama.

Our Own Soap Opera

We had one tenant who had a beautiful child and we both thought she was adorable. The little girl seemed to like me also. While my partner, who had recently become my husband, was talking to the tenants, I would pick up the little girl and she would smooth my hair. She always wanted to kiss me. What was disconcerting was she wanted to put her tongue in my mouth.

These were problem tenants and we were over their place every week trying to collect rent. But every week I got to see the cute little two year old that was stealing my heart. One time when we went over, I asked the girl what her name was. She thought a minute and said, "Fahkah." I knew she had an unusual name, but it didn't seem to be Fahkah.

When I went home and was talking about the child and her name with my husband he such shook his head. That's not her name, and he found it on the lease. "She's saying f#&!er, she thinks her name is f#&!er." I was sick. Later, my husband told me unequivocally that someone was "messing" with that little girl. The next time we were at the tenant's house, I discussed this possibility with the mother and she denied that anything could be happening.

Since the tenants would promise, promise, promise to pay the rent and not deliver; we had to start an eviction. Along with my suspicions of sexual molestation, we called social services and also the police and told them our concerns. To the best of our knowledge both calls went nowhere!

My husband knew I loved the child and he suggested I offer the mother some money to take the girl off her hands. He was certain the tenant would be happy to let the child go for a few thousand dollars or in exchange for free rent. We knew the husband had recently left and that the mother was leaving her kid with strangers so she could go whoring around with other men.

Still, offering to buy someone's child is not an easy subject to broach and we were uncertain about how to do it. We knew we could give this little girl a better life. We could educate her, expose her to music and culture and science, and buy her cute little pink shoes, and love her for the precious little child she was. My husband felt she had been abused beyond repair but was willing to help me raise her, that is, if the mother would agree to part with her child. He also noticed that around me the little girl's demeanor changed into that of a happy, normal child.

When we went back over to the rental, the place was empty except for a bunch of trash. Although the home had been remodeled before the tenants moved in, the walls and carpets were filthy and they had only lived there four months. The beautiful little girl was gone and we never saw her again.

You Don't Have To Be Friends

When a tenant starts becoming a problem, you ultimately have to get rid of them. There are enough good tenants out there that you don't have to put up with their lies, belligerence or disruptive behavior.

On the other hand, you don't have to like your tenants. We had a tenant who I couldn't stand, and my partner had to deal with her. He could tolerate her only slightly better than I could.

When she came to sign the lease, she looked over the unit with her nose in the air. "It's not clean enough to my standards," she said because the stove had some burnt on grease around the edges. "I'll make it work," she grumbled and signed the lease.

Right away she had several complaints, and we sent our contractor over to fix them. She gave him a whole litany of things that she wanted done. He knew to obtain our permission before doing a lot of unnecessary work. He too complained about her unpleasant demeanor. But she paid her rent on time, and after the repairs were completed only called for legitimate purposes.

If you followed the rules of finding a good tenant, you probably won't be dealing with these types of people at all. Possibly you inherited some when you bought the property or let them in before reading this book.

If you thought you followed the rules and still have a problem tenant, look again. Whenever we have a problem tenant, we always look at the five rules to determine where we erred. Always, without fail, we broke one of our own rules, usually the owner was becoming frantic over an empty unit. When you have a problem tenant determine where you went wrong. What clues did you ignore? And why did you ignore them? Were you getting desperate to get the place rented?

Learn from your mistakes.

Chapter Twelve

Getting Tough

Problem tenants have to be handled on an individual basis. You need to weigh the pros and cons of each action and determine a wise strategy before you do anything. Avoid displaying anger or making threats. As a landlord, the courts will hold you to a higher standard than the tenant. You must follow the law exactly, and avoid the temptation to cut off your tenant's water, slash their tires or anything else to make their existence on your property unbearable.

In many states you cannot ask a tenant to move or raise their rent in a way that can be construed as retaliation. Therefore, when you have a tenant causing problems, you will need to proceed with caution. Since state laws vary, educate yourself what is and is not allowed in your state. You may want to consult an attorney on how to proceed. This chapter contains suggestions for dealing with common issues landlords have with tenants. Please note, these are merely suggestions and are not to be considered legal advice.

Communication

Ideally, you could call and discuss the matter with the tenant in a reasonable manner. Sometimes this is impossible if your tenant has turned into a Dr. Jekyll Mr. Hyde sort. Also, you need to keep your own emotions out of the conversation. For those of you with short fuses, it is better to not try to resolve the matter over the phone or in person, as anything you say will be used against you.

When it comes to rental properties, assume that everything you say and do will wind up in court. Most issues are won't—whew! But treating every rental as a potential court case can be a motivator to keep good records, put agreements in writing, and watch what you say and how you say it.

Start a rental journal. This can be set up for both a rent rolls and service log. Every time your tenant telephones notate the date and time of the call and write a few notes about what was said. If your tenant leaves you a message you think may be important later on, make a copy of the recording and keep it. This is especially helpful if the tenant makes threats against you or the property.

Raise the Rent

Again, you may not increase the rent in retaliation against a tenant's demands. Raising rent at the end of the lease, or once a year is legitimate. The rules of how and when to raise rent varies in each state and can be quite nebulous. You will usually have to give a thirty-day notice and sometimes more. Raising the rent above market will raise eyebrows and if the tenant fights it you may end up in court. When you have particularly obnoxious tenants, you may be temped to raise rent significantly -- don't. If the tenants move and you try to re-rent the place for an amount lower than what you raised, the former tenants may have a case against you.

Some states will make the landlord and tenant both sign a statement about the rent increase. Other states don't care. However, your form about the rent increase should also include a statement that says something to the effect of: this will be construed as your thirty-day notice if you fail to abide by the increased rent. Have an attorney help with the exact wording, but make sure the notice is clear so that even someone with poor reading skills can understand.

When you are increasing rent, you may also want to increase the deposit to reflect the raised rent. So if your tenant's deposit was the same as the rent, and you're raising the rent $50 a month, they also need to add $50 toward the deposit. If you collected two month's deposit, the tenants will need to add $100.

With multi-units, the tenants will talk to each other about how much rent they are paying. That means you will have to treat all tenants the same and raise rents accordingly. If you raise your bad tenant ten percent after six months, you will also have to raise your good tenant's rent ten percent in six months. If the good tenants moved into the unit first and you never increased their rent, you will have a very poor case for raising the rent on the tenants who came later.

Enforce the Lease

If raising the rent is not a viable option, now is when your eight page lease as discussed in Chapter 7 will come into play. Before enforcing any provisions of the lease, make sure you as the landlord are completely in compliance with the lease and then see if the tenant is violating it in any way. Unfortunately, enforcing the provisions of the lease will probably upset your tenant even further.

If you have not been collecting late fees and other fees required by the lease, you need to start pestering your tenant to get those paid. Possibly your tenant has accrued some damages, and you can ask them to make those repairs or repay you for the damages they caused. In some states, you can post invoices on the tenant's door itemizing how much is owed and the balance due. Make sure it is facing outward so anyone walking by can see what you have posted, which may be somewhat embarrassing for the tenant.

Once you become serious about enforcement of the lease, your tenant may start threatening to not pay rent or to call the housing authority about all the problems with the house. Keep a log of all the calls, and the gist of the threats. Save all recorded messages from you tenant and record all phone conversations with the tenant. Please note, some states require two party consent in order to record a phone conversation.

Stay calm. Don't worry about the tenant calling the housing authority. Someone from the agency will come out and send you a scary letter with a date to "cure" their list of problems. They will give you plenty of time to get this done, and will often give you an extension if you request it. Usually the repairs need to be taken care of anyway, and they are often minor issues like fixing screens, leaks and putting in another smoke detector. The bad part is some of the items may require pulling a permit -- more money for the city -- and someone from the housing department will need to come back out to approve and sign off on the work.

By the way, we charge all the cost of repairs made because of a call to the housing authority back to the tenant based on the lease they signed giving them three days to tell you of anything not in working order on the premises. That means the screens were fine, the carpet was tacked, the linoleum lay flat, the doors worked and everything was in place when they moved in; therefore, the tenant caused the damages. Exceptions, are leaking roofs, and normal wear of attached appliances like the air conditioner or hot water heater.

Notice To Enter and Inspect Premises

If you suspect the tenant is damaging your property, or even perhaps abandoned it, you can give the tenant a notice to inspect. Different states have different laws about how you may inform the tenant and how much time you must give them. Usually you can post a notice on their main entrance and give them twenty-four to forty-eight hours notice to enter.

While you are conducting the inspection, notate any violations of the lease, damages the tenants have caused or possible illegal activities. Write down and take pictures of what you see. If you have concerns about a tenant who is behaving in a verbally hostile, bring someone with you to stand outside the door while you inspect the house. Err on the side of caution and always make your personal safety a top priority. If the tenant refuses to let you inside, is verbally threatening, or has changed the locks, leave and notate the date, time, and exactly what happened in your rental journal.

Notice To Fix, Cease or Quit

When there is a problem with the exterior of the property, like the tenant isn't mowing their lawn, or they have five cars parked in the back yard, or even getting complaints from neighbors about the traffic and noise – most judges will want you to first have the tenant correct the problem before running to court.

You can post a notice defining the issue, whether it is a violation of the lease or of a local ordinance, and give the tenant a specified amount of time to cure the issue. The time must be reasonable and can range from three days to a month. If you received a notice from the city with a deadline to make the correction, make sure your tenant is aware of the deadline. At the end of the designated time, inspect the property. You may have to post another notice that you will be entering the premises.

If the problem is not fixed, your next step is to begin eviction proceedings.

Notice To Move

Maybe your tenants aren't really doing anything wrong. Perhaps there is something about them that just grates on your nerves. Maybe they call a lot to tell you petty little things that you have no control over like the neighbor's dog is barking, or there's too much traffic on the street. Maybe they complain a lot about things you can control and always want something done. Or maybe you have posted several fix or quit notices and they fix the problem long enough to pass your inspection only to start doing the bad behaviors all over again. For instance, every month you have to remind your tenant according to the lease and they must keep their lawn mowed.

Whatever the reason, if a tenant is becoming unbearable, you should just get rid of them. When you have a month to month lease, you can simply post a notice to terminate tenancy. The length of time varies from state to state, but it is usually thirty days. If your tenant is not month to month, you will have to wait until the term of the lease ends before terminating the tenancy.

Once again, terminating tenancy can be a bit tricky. You can ask or demand that your tenants move for any reason and in most states you do not need to specify why you are asking them to move. On the other hand, in some states, your request for them to move cannot be because of retaliation for repairs or other complaints. However, if your tenants claim you are asking them to move because of retaliation, it is handy to have some legitimate reasons to give to a judge. Avoid coming up with reasons – albeit true – that reflect badly on the tenant. Here are some suggestions:

- You're want to perform extensive upgrades and the place needs to be vacant.

- You have relatives moving into the area and they will be living on your property.

- You're planning to sell.

Unfortunately, anything you tell the judge in a court of law needs to be the truth. Lying can come back and bite you. You may want to consult an attorney on the best way to handle your specific situation. Remember, it is your property and as long as you are not discriminating because of race, color, national origin, sex, disability, familial status, or religion you can have who you want living there.

Notice To Pay or Quit

The easiest and most clear-cut way to get a tenant out is for non-payment of rent. The rental agreement you and the tenant signed, probably has a statement that the rent is due on the first and the date the rent is late. If your lease gives them until the fifth to pay, you will inevitably wait until the fifth until you receive rent, and cannot post a Pay or Quit notice until day six -- another reason not to give tenants half the month to pay.

When a tenant has not paid rent by the due date, on the next day -- regardless of whether the tenant called you or not -- you need to post the notice to Pay or Quit notice. The reason you want to be prompt with your Pay or Quit notices is to reduce the time it takes to evict your tenant.

You can find wording for Pay or Quit notices applicable to your state on the internet. The amount you can claim due on the Pay or Quit notice varies according to state. Most states will allow you to include late and posting fees, other states will only allow you to put the actual rent due. If you cannot include the late and posting charges on the Pay or Quit form, you are still entitled to those fees. When the tenant pays the rent you can remind them of the additional charges.

On the Pay or Quit notice, you will need to explain how long you are giving the tenant, which will be defined by your state. Some states will give a tenant three days to pay the rent, and other states even more time. Alabama gives seven days. No matter how badly you want your tenant to move, you will have to accept rent that comes to you within the period given on the notice to Pay or Quit. However, if the tenant does not have the full amount of rent, and you want them gone, you can refuse to accept it until they have the entire amount. Repeat: you not required to accept partial payment of the rent.

Usually the Pay or Quit notice will guarantee a phone call. This is a good sign, meaning the tenants want to pay the rent. Sometimes a tenant will say they can pay the full rent in the middle of the month. Get an exact date that they are going to pay. Since you are not obligated to start the eviction at the end of the Pay or Quit period, if they do not pay the rent on the date specified, you can begin eviction proceedings.

Other times a tenant will be able to give you a partial payment with promises to pay the rest later. If you want to work with the tenant, you can accept a partial payment .

When you accept a partial payment, immediately give the tenants another Pay or Quit notice for the rest of the rent amount due. They may tell you, they can pay the rest on a certain date. You can tell the tenant you will give them until the date they specified, but if the rent is not paid the following day you will begin eviction proceedings.

If you want your tenant out, you can insist on the full payment amount within the period specified on the Pay or Quit notice. For those tenants who are depositing their rent directly into the bank, you will need to close out that account. This will prevent them from playing the game of putting $10 into the account and forcing you to start all over again with another notice to Pay or Quit.

Here lies the only disadvantage of having tenants pay directly to the bank. Some banks are very good about closing accounts. If an account is closed, it is closed and that is that, no more deposits or other activity is allowed. Other banks will only close an account if there has been no activity for thirty days.

One bank we used had a thirty-day non-activity policy. When the tenants stopped paying rent, we posted a notice to Pay or Quit notice on their door. The tenants did not pay or call in the specified period so we closed the bank account and started eviction proceedings. The day the tenants received the eviction papers, they paid the rent into the closed bank account. When we discovered the bank allowed the deposit, we complained and told the bank manager we would take all our business to another bank if this happened again, he promised to set up something in the system that would completely close any account upon our request.

Some time later, we had another troublesome tenant who was late paying rent. She had a PhD, and a high-paying job, but apparently considered herself too important to bother with paying the rent in a timely manner if at all. We wanted her to go. For the record, every time we had unmarried tenants with a professional or medical doctorate, they caused nothing but problems. Academic credentials and a great job doesn't necessarily transfer to paying the rent on time.

When our hoity-toity PhD tenant was late on rent we posted the Pay or Quit notice. After the timeframe passed, we went to very same bank that promised to keep our accounts closed and closed out her rental account. The tenant put up such a fuss, the teller let her put the money in anyway.

Now we add a statement in large bold print on the notice to Pay or Quit: **The bank account for your rental deposit has been closed.**

If you close the account, or say you did, on the Pay or Quit notice you will need to explain alternatives for the rent to be paid. One option is for them to call you and make arrangements to pick up the rent in person. If you allow them to mail the rent to you, make sure the address – your post office box and not home address -- is clearly stated on the notice. Some courts may consider any postmark dated within the Pay or Quit timeframe as received.

We recommend working as much as possible with tenants who are struggling to pay the rent. Many times, tenants are one paycheck away from homelessness. If something happens – their car breaks down, they are off work due to an illness – they simply will not have the money to pay the rent. When these tenants call and inform you of the situation and tell you how they are going to get you paid, you can work with them. However, you must get rid of those tenants who don't call, lie, or try to manipulate you out of paying the rent.

Chapter Thirteen
Evictions

Evictions are a part of owning rental properties. What usually happens is either you are new to the game and are in the make-a-lot-of-mistakes-about-selecting-tenants phase or you have been trying to rent your vacancy for so long you lower your standards. Finally, someone came around who wanted to rent your place, and even though they wouldn't be your first pick, they were your only pick. Now that they are causing trouble and failing to pay the rent, you wished you had waited.

Evictions are more costly than vacancies, so it is better to held back for a quality tenant. Every time we have to do an eviction we review the screening process as described in Chapters 3 and 4 to see where we went wrong.

When buying rental investment properties it is important to include vacancies and evictions in your ownership budget. As property managers, we often took over someone else's headache, which meant we had to assess the situation and start the eviction on the owner's behalf.

Other common reasons for evictions is that something negative happens in the tenant's life. They lose a job, they are in an accident and don't have insurance, they go off their psychotropic medication, or they start doing drugs. There is no way you can account for any of this, you can screen for some of it, but in life there are no guarantees.

Eviction laws vary from state to state. In spite of popular belief, in California's non-rent control areas, you can get tenants out rather quickly. And contrary to what you might think, evictions in less than tenant friendly states like Alabama take forever. Go figure.

Posting the Eviction Notice

Although the forms and timelines vary, the procedure for an eviction is similar in every state. As explained in the last chapter, you will need to post a Pay or Quit notice as required by the state giving the tenant a specified time, place, and amount to pay the rent.

Since the Pay or Quit notice is a legal document, make sure it is properly worded. States have different rules a landlord must follow, so obey the laws in your state to the letter. A Pay or Quit notice that does not contain the required information or is incorrectly worded may cause a judge to rule that you must start the entire eviction process over again.

You can deliver or post this notice yourself, but when you are serious about an eviction, you will need to have proof of posting. In theory before posting any notice on the door you must knock or ring the doorbell and wait a reasonable amount of time before taping the notice to the door. A reasonable amount of time is not clearly defined. Ring, knock, repeat, count to thirty, and tape the notice securely to the door.

You want to make sure you post the notice on a commonly used entrance, like the front door, and if legal in your state have the notice facing outward so anyone passing by can see the tenants are about to be evicted. Tape it on all four sides and corners so it cannot easily be torn off or blown away by the wind. For additional proof of delivery, you can take a photograph of the notice on the door. Some states will require you to also send the tenants a copy of the Pay or Quit notice in the mail if it was not delivered in person. You may want to send it certified or at least get a proof of mailing to show the courts you have complied with the law.

Rarely do tenants ever "quit" the premises. Maybe if the posting said "Three Days to Pay Rent or Move Out" tenants would better understand what is being asked of them and actually move before forcing you to start an eviction. But the legal wording is quit, and it seems tenants understand very clearly if they don't pay the rent and eviction is soon to follow, yet tend to stay and hunker down until they know the sheriff is coming.

The law is very particular about when the specified time begins on these postings. Usually the day of the posting does not count as day one, even if you post early in the morning. Day one begins the following day. Sometimes states do not clarify if the timeframe is in calendar days, business days, or workdays. Assume business days, and give the tenant extra time because courts are notorious for ruling against landlords for minor infractions. The final day to pay must be a business day. For example, if you post a three-day notice on Thursday, you will not be able to start eviction until Tuesday because the third day ended on Sunday and was not a business day. Therefore, the tenant gets one more day to pay. If Monday happens to be a holiday you will have to wait until Wednesday before going further.

During this time you must give the tenant a chance to correct the problem or pay their rent in full. If you want the tenant gone, do not accept partial payment. Once a partial payment of rent is accepted, you have to start the process all over again.

Unlawful Detainer Action

When the time period for the Pay or Quit notice is over, you can file an unlawful detainer action. An unlawful detainer action is a document filed with the court that starts the legal process of eviction. The document will give the tenant a specified amount of time answer the complaint ranging from five to fourteen days, or even more. States vary widely as to what occurs next and how much time is given. Here's how the unlawful detainer action can very from state to state:

- Called something else
- One or two pages to over ten pages
- May be self-explanatory to fill out or very legalistic
- Different amount of times for tenant to answer or move
- May allow additional time to answer after the expiration
- May have service for possession and money due on one document
- May require service for possession separate from the money collection
- Different processing serving rules

Once the form is filled out you will need to make at least one copy and take the original and photocopies to the county clerk to have it recorded. Some clerks will look over the document carefully and if they find errors make you correct them before recording the document. The clerk will stamp the document and give you a copy to deliver to your tenants.

Remember, court clerks are not allowed to give legal advice, they generally give the document a brief scan and you won't find out it you made errors until the judge dismisses your case because the form was not filled out correctly. If you are uncertain how to fill out the form you may want to hire an attorney, paralegal or eviction service to help you. Accuracy is paramount.

Process Servers

You want the unlawful detainer served as soon as possible, as the clock only starts after the tenant is served.

Since you are an interested party, you may *not* serve the unlawful detainer complaint. If you have more than one person on the lease, they each will need to be served. You can call a process server or have the sheriff to serve the document. Most states will allow any disinterested party who is of legal age to do the service. Sometimes you can find a friend to help you get the document served. A friend might be cheaper and faster, but your friend may also have to come to court and testify exactly when and how they served the document. Better to pay a process server than to put such an imposition on a friend.

It may be tempting to use the sheriff to serve the document because a person in uniform with a gun tends to be intimidating, and the sheriff is usually cheaper than a process server. Before committing to the sheriff, find out how long it will take them to get the document out for service. In many jurisdictions it could take weeks before they will even make the first effort to serve the document.

For delivering the Unlawful Detainer Action, process servers are usually the best choice. Process servers are bonded, know the rules of service, and will be believed in court.

A good process server will be out without twenty-four hours after receiving the filing. Unfortunately, many process servers treat their occupation as a Monday through Friday nine-to-five job. As in every occupation, some process servers are better than others. The bad ones may go to the location a few times and simply give up and they may or may not notify you.

The tenants know service is coming and are going to do what they can to avoid it. That being the case, you will need to find a good process server who is aggressive and will get the job done. Until you find a reliable process server you will have to follow-up, sometimes daily with the one you are using.

Most of our process servers have been so-so. Although they do get the job done faster than the sheriff, they still tend to sit on the complaint for a few days or charge more if you want them to go out immediately.

We had one process server in California who was excellent. Rather than partying and having fun on a Saturday night, she followed one of our tenants to their place of employment and served him in the restaurant where he worked. She reported back he wasn't too happy that his supervisor and co-workers witnessed him being served. But he had refused to answer the door when he was at home, what did he expect? When tenants don't pay rent, we don't have a lot of sympathy if they are embarrassed when the process service arrives.

Give your process server as much information as you can regarding the whereabouts of your tenant to help ensure a prompt and speedy service. This is where your application comes in handy, you should be able to give the process server information about where the tenants work, and names of the friends and relatives listed under "Emergency Contacts." Keep in mind many states require each individual on the lease must be served.

If you cannot get your tenants served, individual states have their own rules to remedy this situation. Most states will allow certified mail to be considered service -- but only if the receiver signed for the letter. People know certified mail is bad and will not pick up the letter. Some states may require a court adjudication before allowing certified mail, but once adjudicated a certified letter is considered service whether the tenant picks it up or not.

After your tenants are served, they have a specified amount of time to answer the claim against them. If your tenants don't answer, all you need to do is obtain a Writ of Execution. This means more paperwork to fill out and more court costs. In some jurisdictions the county clerk will be able to stamp and approve the forms, which takes only a few minutes not counting travel time and standing in line. In other jurisdictions the paperwork will have to be approved by a judge. This means submitting paperwork and waiting until the judge "gets around to it," which could take weeks.

Evictions are not urgent matter for judges, so they do not make this type of paperwork a priority. If you are doing an eviction over a holiday season, there is a strong possibility the judge will wait until the holiday over before acting. Forget your fantasy of the sheriff coming and putting the deadbeats out on Christmas Day.

More bad news, some jurisdictions allow tenants to appeal the writ. The good news however, is the appeal will not delay execution of the writ, they will still have to move at the behest of the sheriff, even if their appeal date is after that time.

Eviction Services/Attorneys

Some states have additional forms that must be filed in order to complete the eviction. For instance California has a Pre-Judgment Claim Right to Possession which is a document ensuring everyone in the property is out. This form is filed with the Unlawful Detainer Action and it is very important that you have wording which indicates everyone at the property whether they are named on the lease or not is removed. Some jurisdictions will allow you to list the tenants on the lease and include the tag line: all tenants, sub-tenants and *all others.* Find out what your state requires to guarantee every individual in the rental is removed.

If you do not do this correctly, one of your tenant's friends could be in the house, and not be forced to leave. They could then allow your wayward tenants back in, and you would have to start the whole eviction process all over again.

If you are inexperienced in these matters, you should hire an eviction service or an attorney to file the paperwork. Many judges are pro-tenant, and will use a minor mistake on the paperwork as an excuse to force you to start the eviction all over again.

The problem with using attorneys is they generally charge too much and like to make federal cases out of simple evictions. Generally attorneys do not care about a quick eviction or that you are losing money, and it is in their interest to make sure the tenant answers. Before we knew how to file our own legal paperwork, one hundred percent of the tenants answered the Unlawful Detainer Action that had been processed using an attorney. When we filed on our own about sixty percent answered. Therefore, make sure you keep copies of everything the attorney or eviction service filed. Now you have a template if you want to do the eviction yourself the next time.

Answer

The Unlawful Detainer Action will give the tenant a specified amount of time to answer. Tenants answer because it gives them more time, and often they genuinely believe they have a legitimate reason to not pay rent. They usually go to legal aid to help with the answer and will give some bogus reason for not paying the rent. A favorite claim is the place is uninhabitable, although for some reason the tenants continue to live there. Tenants will try every trick in the book to delay and stay. What they are aiming for is more time.

Even if you are experienced with the paperwork segment of the eviction process, you may want to hire an attorney when a tenant answers. Call several attorneys and hire the one who won't try and make the eviction into a convoluted legal procedure. Eviction for non-payment of rent is rarely a complicated matter. Your tenants haven't paid the rent -- that's it -- they have to go. Of course, evictions for reasons other than non-payment of the rent can be a little sticky.

We have had attorneys who have tried to gouge us for eviction services. After sending the documents over, they wanted to bill us a $500 reading fee. We didn't fall for it, and you shouldn't either. Evictions for non-payment of the rent are all state code and not case law, therefore a simple matter.

The price you pay for the attorney should only be for an hour or two of their time. If an attorney is charging you more than that, they are cheating you. The eviction process can be intimidating however, and any missteps can send you back to square one so a good attorney is worth every penny.

We had a great eviction attorney in California who only charged $300 to show up to court and ask the tenant when they would be out. We were able to handle all the court documents and just needed an attorney to show up in court. We were spoiled.

In Alabama all the attorneys insisted on working the entire process and charged around $2000. We met an attorney fresh out of law school trying to find her footing and told her our eviction needs. Although she wanted to go into a different area of law, she was having trouble getting established. She saw a gold mine and started doing evictions for a fraction of the price all the other attorneys in town were charging. Needless to say her business grew rapidly and she confessed to my partner and me that the other attorneys in town were very upset with her actions. Many of them were writing her letters threatening a lawsuit, and some letters were just threatening. She wasn't concerned. Find someone like her.

No matter what the tenants' charges are against you, they will have to prove them. You may need to bring your receipts of repairs to court and also your rental journal where you kept track of all their phone calls. If you have been diligently reporting all your ingoing and outgoing calls, your journal will create dramatic proof that the tenants never complained about the issues. When a tenant does call you about an issue and leaves a message, always try to save those messages.

You also need to remember, according the lease, the tenants had three days after moving in to notify you of any issues with the property. Since you were not notified, that means the tenants caused the destruction and must pay for it themselves. Failure to make repairs is not a reason to not pay the rent, although in a tenant's point of view, it seems fair and reasonable. It is futile to argue the point with the tenant, even if you read them the statute, they will not believe you. They have a friend or cousin who took a law class, and by-golly, if you haven't made repairs, they don't have to pay rent. Most states allow the tenant to make the repairs themselves and take that amount off the rent, but to simply not pay because repairs haven't been made does not comply with the law nor with the lease they freely signed.

If the tenants are holding rent for a legitimate reason, most courts will require them to show that they have the ability to pay the rent in full up to the day of court and may have to put the funds in a court escrow account.

On court day, a good attorney will discuss the matter with the tenant and explain to them they have to move even if repairs have not been made. Since they heard it from an attorney, they will understand their claim of the place being uninhabitable won't work. Even if the tenant brings their own attorney, your lawyer will ask the tenants when they can be out, and explain to them moving is the only choice. If the tenant wants to stay and has the money, it is still your property and if you want them gone you can have them go. Although the tenants may have been totally disagreeable and obnoxious with you and have made horrible threats, they usually become compliant with the attorney. The judge will formalize the agreement between tenant and attorney/owner, and a writ of execution will be issued.

If no agreement can be made, the case will go before a judge. Each side will have a chance to present their testimony so be sure and bring evidence for everything you are alleging including proof of service. Regardless of the tenant's sob story the judge needs to abide by the law. Usually the judge will ascertain if the tenants were given legal service and the documents are filled out correctly, then rule. As long as you abided by the law, and the tenant does not have a legitimate claim, the judge should rule in your favor.

Sheriff

After you have your ruling, it still takes more time to oust your tenants. You will obtain a Writ of Execution, which goes to the sheriff and they will follow its orders. Usually the Writ will have a date by which the tenants need to be gone. If they have not vacated the property by the court ordered date, you will be able to have the sheriff come out and get rid of them. You will probably have to pay another fee for this service.

Different jurisdictions work in various ways. In some states, the tenant has no notice of when the sheriff will arrive. In other states, the sheriff will first post a notice giving the tenant warning that they are coming. Usually this is enough to get them out, but not always.

You will have to coordinate with the sheriff when they will be at the property to supervise the eviction. The sheriff will schedule a time that is convenient for them – not you – to come out and do the eviction. In some counties the sheriff will do evictions only on certain days of the week like Tuesday and Thursday. Other counties, the sheriff will come whenever they feel like it, and you may even have to beg and plead with the sheriff to come out and do their job – seriously. In Alabama the sheriff would not come if there was a thirty percent chance or more of rain. Sometimes you will be lucky to receive an hour's notice before the sheriff arrives. You do not need to be at the property when the sheriff arrives, but a responsible adult will have to witness and sign the sheriff's documents. This is your day of reckoning, so coming to the eviction party is always a good idea.

You will definitely need to bring a locksmith and have all the locks rekeyed on the property so the evictees cannot regain admittance. In fact, if you cannot be present, the locksmith can sign the sheriff's documentation. After the sheriff has removed the tenants – sometimes by gunpoint – and the tenants return to the property, it will now be considered trespassing and/or breaking and entering. You won't have to go through another eviction.

States handle tenants belongings in a couple of ways.

Good states will allow you to hire some movers, or haulers, or friends to put all the tenant's belongings out on the front yard while the sheriff is present. The movers cannot put anything on the sidewalk or street. You can help them if you like. You must have a fast-working crew. The sheriff may give you less than an hour to get all the tenant's belongings removed, that means no one needs to take any special care to preserve any of your evicted tenant's stuff. You won't have time to carefully wrap dishes or other breakable items. In fact, if you accidentally happened to combine open and broken jars of food in with nice clothes, it would certainly be considered part of the rush to get everything completed. We highly recommend that you do not purposely cause any damage to the evictee's property. While the sheriff is present, the tenants may not re-enter the rental. They will have to stand outside and watch their stuff thrown and tossed out like garbage on the front lawn.

When all their junk is out, neighbors and strangers can pick through and take their belongings. Whatever is left after twenty-four hours will have to be hauled away at your expense.

Other pro-tenant states will require the landlord hold onto the tenant's possessions for fourteen days. You can pack their stuff up and hold it in storage, which is expensive to do, or you can simply keep the stuff at the property. If they tenant has property left in the house, you will need to board up the windows to keep the tenant from breaking in. If they do not claim their property in fourteen days (or whatever amount of time specified by the state) you can have it hauled away, sell it, or do whatever you want. In these states, if the tenant wants their property back, you can charge them a storage fee. Charge them the cost of unpaid rent, court costs and attorney fees and a couple of hundred extra for all your trouble. They'll usually let their stuff go.

Now that the tenants are gone, you can assess damages and get the place ready to rent. Total all of your estimates or actual repair costs, legal fees, lost rent, and other expenses to send over to a collection agency or attorney. Eventually a good collector will get you some of your money back. You can sue for your costs, but the court may not allow for all your claims and you will still end up sending it to collections. The only thing suing a tenant will do is indicate they have a judgment against them on their credit report.

Use a collection agency that will report the tenants' debt on their credit report. Don't hold your breath about recouping any costs; but every once in a while you'll receive some unexpected money. Basically, what the tenant did to you cannot be recovered. Claim the expenses as a loss on your taxes and move on.

After the eviction, analyze where you went wrong in the application process that you brought in a bunch of losers. Did you follow our advice to the letter? Did you adequately check out the references? Were you desperate? Were you manipulated? What did your instincts tell you about these people that you ignored? Thoroughly analyze where you went wrong to avoid making the same mistake again. Think of your mistakes as education, a good education is very expensive, but it is worth the cost.

Chapter Fourteen
True Eviction Stories

For the most part evictions are a matter of waiting and pretty dull stuff. The tenants haven't paid the rent, you go through the legal process, when the sheriff comes the tenants are usually gone – but not always. The following stories are absolutely true. We changed the names of the tenants and others involved to keep the anonymity of the guilty parties who were eventually evicted.

Have a Blessed Day

We had a tenant who was very obnoxious. Cindy wanted things fixed, but would never be around for the handyman to come inside and do the repairs. She didn't understand that these workers had other things to do besides work around her schedule. Cindy also did not want anyone in her house while she was not home, including ourselves. In fact, she left a nasty message saying she was the only one who should have a key, and we the owners weren't even entitled to one. One of Cindy's messages was a ten-minute rant full of ultimatums and threats that ended with, "Have a blessed day."

Cindy also stopped paying her rent. How surprising is that? We started an eviction. She called the housing department. We received an official letter from them listing several items that needed to be repaired at the house, most of them nonsense. In the meantime, the eviction was proceeding. We filed the unlawful detainer action ourselves but needed someone to serve it. In the past, we used the sheriff and they took too long, so we hired a process server.

We had planned a nine day cruise, a well-deserved vacation, and simply assumed the process server would get Cindy served while we were gone and most of her grace period would be over by the time we returned. Since we were on a ship out of the country, we were out of phone service range. Upon arriving home, we called the process server to find out the date Cindy was served.

The process server we hired also claimed to be a private detective, and he told us he thought Cindy must have moved and wanted to know where she was working so he could serve her there. The tenant had changed jobs during her tenancy and never informed us of her new place of work. In spite of what the detective told us, we were certain Cindy still lived at the property. In order to confirm this, we drove by the rental property where Cindy was now living rent-free for over a month, and it was obvious to us *non*-detectives she was still in the house. The biggest clue was her lawn furniture remained outside on the patio.

Calling the process server back, we told him Cindy was still living at the house. He insisted she had moved. That afternoon we asked another one of our good tenants if she would like to make some extra money, drove her over to the house and she posted the form for possession. Service complete -- 15 minutes.

Driving by the house the following day, we saw the notice had been removed from the front door.

Hmm, the professional detective was wrong. Cindy was still living there.

She called and told us she would move. She left the place fairly clean, but her form of revenge was to cut all the wires: the phone, cable and heat wires. We also had to make the repairs for the city and have them inspect the place before any new tenants could move in.

Drugs Change People

One of the houses we were managing had a tenant who started using drugs. Bonny was a young single mother and seemed very responsible. For several months, she paid the rent on the spot and in many ways was an ideal tenant.

However as time progressed, Bonny started paying the rent late, making partial payments, failing to call, and failing to be home when she said we could pick up the rent. Then she completely stopped paying. She ignored the Pay or Quit Notices we were now posting on her door with increasing regularity and we had no choice but to start eviction proceedings.

Bonny answered the Unlawful Detainer Action, saying the house was uninhabitable. We called in our attorney who was a single male slightly older than the Bonny. She used her feminine wiles on the attorney to convince him she would pay the rent and get caught up. We agreed to this because it would be written in the court order. If Bonny failed to do as promised, the writ would go to the sheriff and she would be out right away. She would also be paying rent directly to the court and not us.

Of course, Bonny didn't pay as she promised, so we had the sheriff come out. First, they posted the five-day notice warning when they would be out. In the interim she vacated the property, but gave the house keys to her druggie friends who trashed the place. There were holes in the walls, the carpet ruined and gang graffiti everywhere. It took over $3000 to repair the damages.

We later found out she was in jail on drug charges.

The Eviction From Hell

The eviction from hell took over six months to resolve, we learned every aspect of an eviction. This eviction inspired us to start our own eviction service as an adjunct to the property management firm and began taking over other people's tenant problems.

We rented a unit of a duplex to the nicest couple, Ralph and Diane. Their daughter was very withdrawn, but other than that everything seemed fine. We were still relatively new to property management and didn't realize withdrawn children as a sign of potential problems. For the first six months, however, Ralph and Diane were fairly good tenants. Although often late, one of them would call to tell us the rent would be in by the end of the month. And they would eventually pay.

Then their tardiness grew worse. Diane told us her husband had lost his job due to a work injury and once he found another one they would be back on track. When we talked to Ralph, he had a different story. His story didn't make any sense and he rambled on and on about being a prophet of Jesus. Needless to say, he didn't find another job. Since he had seemed normal when we rented to them, we thought he possibly had gotten off his mentally stabilizing medication.

Around this time, the tenant in the other unit needed some work done, but the repair person couldn't access a water valve. The necessary valve was in Ralph and Diane's duplex, but they refused to give the plumber entrance. We called asked what was going on and ordered them to give the plumber access. They said they would, but they didn't want him inside their house, which is always a clue something is terribly wrong. Well then, just let him in the backyard.

As with our other tenants, Ralph and Diane were paying their rent by going to the bank. They started pulling the trick of putting a few dollars in the account to force us to start the eviction process all over from scratch. Usually we have individual accounts for each property, but this one was a shared account with the property owner and we were dependent on her to close the bank account.

The owner dragged her heels and it took another month to get the account closed. When the rental account was finally closed, we posted another Pay or Quit notice and told them no partial payments would be accepted. Now they could no longer go to the bank, and they went to their second strategy -- which, obviously was not to pay any rent.

When they could no longer pull their $20 rent payment trick, we received a nasty fax from the tenants stating that the house was inhabitable due to repairs not being done. They claimed they had called on three different occasions wanting repairs and we had not responded. This is where a phone log comes in handy. We had no record or recollection of any phone calls. If a tenant calls about a repair, we get it taken care of promptly.

Another clue that Ralph and Diane were making false repair accusations was that they stated the problem was with "old rusty pipes." That didn't make sense. First of all, the property wasn't that old. Second, it was a duplex and the people in the other unit didn't have any rusty pipe problem. Regardless, we called a plumber to go out and tell us what was needed.

We posted another notice on the door stating that we had called a plumber and gave the date he would be out to look at the pipe problem. We also noticed that they had changed the locks on the security screen so it no longer had a doorknob, but required two keys to unlock and pull the door open.

The plumber came and reported back to us. At first they didn't want to let him in, but finally did. Ralph was very belligerent with him and followed him around the house threatening to call 911. The plumber looked at the problem, it had some slow drainage, wasn't hurting anything and would cost $165 to repair. The plumber didn't want to fix it, because he was kind of afraid of the tenant. We asked him to give us all this information in writing, which he did.

We had Ralph and Diane served with the unlawful detainer action, which took forever because they were avoiding service. The process server had served the wife easily enough, but the husband seemed to be a paranoid schizophrenic and would never open the door. However, the process server had a secret weapon. She sent out a cute young woman to serve the process and Ralph opened the door.

At that point, the owner thought maybe we should just get an attorney to take care of the rest of the eviction. We called some attorneys on her behalf and they wanted to charge $2000 for an eviction. Too high.

The owner suggested we call some eviction services. So we found one who was also an attorney and would do the whole thing for $500. We tried to explain to him all that was needed to do was to wait for an answer. He took the job and the money, went to court and stopped the case so he could start it all over again from scratch.

We could have killed him and the owner. The tenants were now a little wiser about avoiding process and the attorney who cancelled our case couldn't get them served. It had been months now, and the tenants were living on the property rent-free. Finally the owner decided to just let us handle it, so we fired the attorney took the paperwork and gave it to our process server who petitioned the court to allow service by certified mail.

By now the tenants were confused. They answered the first process, which had been canceled by the eviction attorney, and didn't answer the second process which came by certified mail. We went to the court and got the writ, thinking the eviction would soon be over.

Wrong. Ralph and Diane appealed the writ, claiming they had not been properly served. They wanted their day in court, they were supposedly living in uninhabitable conditions. If the conditions are uninhabitable -- move! Or make the repairs and take it off the rent, but a tenant cannot simply refuse to pay rent and expect to live at the property rent-free.

In addition to uninhabitable conditions, Ralph and Diane also claimed that we were charging unfair rent and it should be $700 a month instead of $900 a month. They claimed the rent was far above market value, even though the tenant in the adjoining mirror image unit was paying more rent than they were.

Speaking of the tenant next door, she was starting to call and complain to us about her nutty neighbors. She told us that Ralph was crazy and would harass her whenever she went outside. He was also bothering her children accusing them of spying. She was afraid of Ralph. We asked her to bear with us, we were evicting as fast as possible, but the legal process was creating a comedy of errors. She could not wait, and we lost a good tenant because of the time it took to get Ralph and Diane out.

The courts were more than happy to grant the appeal to the Ralph and Diane who had not paid any rent for nearly six months now. Half a year, rent free, such a deal.

To make matters worse, the tenants also filed a small claims suit against us personally for the maximum amount allowed which was $5000 at the time. Great.

Because Ralph and Diane answered the complaint, we had to call in an attorney to represent our interests in court. All the eviction attorneys we called wanted to turn the eviction into a federal case and were charging way too much money. We called our attorney who did our evictions in another county of the same state and asked if he would be willing to come out and represent us. He could have cared less that we filled out and filed our own paperwork, never tried to gouge us with attorney fees and didn't make a big deal out of a simple eviction. We told him we would put him up in a five star hotel and buy him a great dinner plus pay him his gas and usual expenses. He didn't want that, but would charge us more. Okay. Instead of $300 he charged $450. Sure beats $2000. He came to court, asked Ralph and Diane when they would be out. They agreed to be out on the fifteenth of next month, and that was that.

Well, not exactly. On the fifteenth, Ralph and Diane were still living on the premises. Time to call in the sheriff. The sheriff posted the five-day notice and we made arrangements for the locksmith to be present for the eviction. Usually when tenants get the five-day notice that the sheriff is coming, they'll leave. Since Ralph and Diane had already promised to be gone, we thought they would be out before the sheriff came.

We were wrong. The sheriff knocked and rang the doorbell, no one answered. The locksmith had to pick the locks in order to get inside. Ralph and Diane were still living at the place, hiding in the garage, and the sheriff had to bring them out by gunpoint!

Finally they were gone. We had to board up the windows to keep them out.

The small claims lawsuit against us was still lingering. We were out of town on the date specified and asked for an extension. It was denied. We asked again for an extension, this time sending proof we were out of town and also explaining that the tenants were evicted and no longer in the property. The extension was granted.

When the court day came, we thought, maybe since Ralph and Diane were living in another place for over two months, they would just not show up to court. But nope, they were there. While we were sitting listening to the judge tell everyone how the small claims process worked, he said something that made the tenants realize, they would lose their case. For any dollar amount that they were asking for, they had to show proof such as receipts. Of course, the tenant who had lived rent free for over half a year had none of that. We, on the other hand, had plenty of receipts, a letter from a plumber stating how belligerent the tenant had been, a letter from the contractor who fixed up the place afterwards that said all it needed was a few cosmetic repairs (i.e. the place was habitable all along), and the eviction papers.

Before going in front of the judge, parties are given one last chance to discuss their charges with each other. Ralph told us was he didn't want $5000, he just didn't want an eviction on their record. We hashed through the process and came up with a deal.

Afterwards, we couldn't believe it. Ralph and Diane seemed like the nicest, reasonable couple, and based solely on their behavior people we would enjoy renting to. Go figure.

Even without an eviction on their record, based upon the application a savvy landlord should know not to rent to them. First, Ralph and Diane would not have a questionable rental history. Second, since he was out of work for a year, he would not have a solid work history. Finally, their child was too withdrawn.

Chapter Fifteen

Deposit Return

Ideally a tenant will give you a thirty-day notice of their intent to move. Some do some don't. When tenants give you notice they are leaving, they are probably expecting their deposit back. Ask for their new address so you can send it there.

The purpose behind a thirty-day notice is so you can market the property and have a new tenant move in without a vacancy period. Of course, while a tenant is around with all their stuff, the place will not look the best. In addition, tenants don't like the idea of strangers coming to where they live to look around. Therefore, it is better to wait until the tenant is completely gone to show the place. Still, it is good to put the thirty-day notice in the lease because most tenants don't give proper notice and it becomes a legitimate reason not to return the deposit.

Different states have different time limits to return a deposit. California only gives a landlord twenty-one days, which forces the landlord to get right on the matter. Other states have a lengthier period and you can often get the property rented again before having to send back the deposit and/or the letter of explanation as to why the tenant is not receiving their deposit back. Make sure you sent the final accounting within the state's required time allowance or you may be subject to penalties if the tenant pursues the matter.

The exact date a tenant left can be nebulous. Some people believe that tenants are considered to inhabit the unit until they surrender keys, not necessarily true. Check and see what your state laws say regarding this matter. Our experience has been that the issue is not addressed in the statutes or is very vague. In addition our experience has been non-rent payers do not return keys.

We had tenants who believed they inhabited the property until the keys were returned. Sounds reasonable on the surface. These particular tenants had an issue with the place and vacated the month after moving in. We heard a litany of complaints and knew they would be leaving but were not given an exact date.

At the beginning of the month when the rent was not paid, we stopped the by the property and posted a three day pay or quit notice. Three days later, we went by the property and saw the notice had been removed. The front room blinds were open, and we peeked inside. The place was empty so we entered. The tenants had left a dirty mess.

While we were there, one of the tenants stopped by and demanded to know what we were doing in her house. Wait a minute, we had posted a pay or quit, rent had not been paid, the place was empty, that meant the tenants were gone. She did not quite see it that way and insisted we could not access the property until she returned the keys. We refused to be intimidated.

Tenants do not always tell you when they are leaving neither do they always return keys. Sometimes a tenant will simply abandon the property. More often a tenant will inform you they are out and tell you where they left the keys. Other times a tenant will tell you they will be out by the end of the month, and you never hear another peep so you are not exactly certain when they are gone.

If a tenant is very clear when they will be gone, you can simply enter the premises and assess any damages and necessary repairs. However, you may have a tenant who you have not been able to contact by phone and are not certain if they have vacated or not. You can post a notice to enter the premises. On the notice state the reason for inspection and the date, which will be based upon the amount of time your state requires tenant notification for entering the property. Usually if the tenants are still living in the home, they will call and tell you they are still there. Otherwise, on the date specified on the notice, enter the premises to see if they have moved.

We had a tenant who was the single mother of three children. The mother became very ill and her brother moved her into a nursing home. He took responsibility of the children and vaguely mentioned being out at the end of the month. He did not return the keys.

At the end of the month, we went to the place thinking they were gone only to find a house full of furniture. We weren't sure if the tenant's brother was intending to come back for the rest of the furniture and household items or not. We posted a seven-day notice to Pay or Quit, and saw it was still on the front door on day seven, a sign the family had not returned. We entered the property, and the furniture was still there exactly as before. We assumed they were permanently gone.

You cannot charge them for rekeying, if a tenant returns the keys, but do charge them if the keys were not returned.

After a tenant moves, and before a new tenant moves in, rekey all exterior locks for safety reasons. You cannot be certain how many copies of the keys the tenant made and who has possession of those keys.

Unless a tenant still has a key and continues to enter the property – this has happened – you can wait to rekey when all the work is done. The reason to wait is that you may have to give out the key to the handyman or other people who are doing some of the fix-up work. When you wait until after all the work is done, your tenant can be secure that no one else besides yourself has a key to their place.

Usually tenants don't abandon their stuff, but they will often leave behind a bunch of junk. You will have to haul it away.

Add the cost of hauling to the tenant's bill and deduct from the deposit. Once the tenants and all their junk are gone, you will need to assess damages. If it appears the tenants purposely damaged your place with holes in the walls and other destruction going beyond the deposit, consider filing charges against them.

Be careful to distinguish between damages and reasonable wear and tear. As a rule of thumb if something needs to be replaced, it was damaged; otherwise consider it reasonable wear and tear. You also cannot charge tenants for repairs that you failed to perform that caused more damage, such as from a leaking roof. However, if you were not informed of a repair and by the tenant's failure to notify you of the problem the damages were made worse, you could possibly make a claim they owe you for the additional damages.

Maybe you rented out a dirty place and the tenant accepted the place as-is and left the place. In this case, you don't get to charge for cleaning. However, if you and the tenant agreed that you would give them money off the rent so the tenant could clean the place instead of you doing the work; you have a justification that the place was in effect clean when they moved in and can charge for cleaning. If the stove and oven were clean and grease free when they moved in, and it was dirty when they left, you can charge for cleaning. On the other hand, carpet cleaning, cannot be deducted and is attributed to normal wear and tear. Stains and cigarette burns would be considered damage.

If your lease specified that the tenants would take care of the lawn and you now have dirt instead of grass, you can deduct replacement costs off their deposit. But if the lawn is not in pristine condition – too bad – normal wear and tear. Unless the tenants left the weeds a foot high, mowing doesn't count.

You can find charts and information online specifying the different between wear and tear and damages. Before starting any work take photographs of the damages. Make sure anyone examining the photos will see the actually damage and not just a dirty wall.

Even though you intend to do a lot of the work yourself, ask for a professional cleaning service to come out and give you estimates to make your property spotless. Get a lawn company out and tell you how much it is going to cost to bring the yard back the way it was, and a contractor to give you estimates for all the damages the tenant caused.

Once you have all your estimates in writing, you need to write a letter to the tenant regarding their deposit. First subtract any unpaid late/posting fees that the tenant has not paid. Then subtract all the estimates to bring the property back to the condition at the time the tenants moved in not including normal wear and tear. Write a check out for the balance.

Often your costs will be more than what was covered by the deposit. In this case, the tenant owes you money. Reflect this amount in the letter to the tenant and tell them you expect to be paid for these costs. Include copies of the estimates with your letter.

If you know the tenant's new address, you don't need to send the final accounting through certified mail. However, you may want to get a proof of mailing just for your own peace of mind. When the tenant has not given you a forwarding address, mail it to their last known address (your property) and send it certified.

When a tenant received their full or partial deposit back, you are done with them. About one hundred percent of the time, if a tenant owes you money, they probably are not going to reimburse you. Send your bill to a good collection agency to try and recoup some of your costs. You may decide to take your tenants to court and obtain a judgment against them. You will likely receive your judgment but will still have to send the bill to collections. In addition, the judge may not allow all your costs. So we forget the courts and sent everything straight to collections.

Many landlords do not bother trying to collect these expenses knowing it is mostly an exercise in futility. You'll never completely recoup your costs. True. Eventually you may receive a few dollars here and there, but you will never regain all your costs.

Nevertheless, we still send the bill to collections. It is not so much about the money as training tenants to be better people. Deadbeat tenants who owe you money, and damaged your property deserve to be hounded and made miserable by bill collectors. What's more a good collection agency will put the tenant's bill on a credit report. Property managers who look at credit will see this and refuse to rent to them. When tenants realize there are repercussions for their actions they might actually learn to become more responsible people.

Chapter Sixteen

Adventures in Property Management

By now you should realize that being a landlord entails a lot more than sitting back and collecting rent. If you are managing your own properties you will confront issues you never dreamed of. You may become jaded like a cop and forever change your viewpoint on humanity.

Some of your tenants will create an ongoing drama that is more interesting than any soap opera on TV. Tenants will try and drag you into their petty arguments, they will try and get you to take sides, and of course, they will threaten to sue you for every penny you have.

Because of all the problems and legal hassles, property management, it is never, ever dull. The purpose of this chapter is to tell true stories about some of our more unusual experiences in managing properties. These stories were part of our day-to-day aspects of being a landlord.

Bats

One day the tenant of a property we managed called in a panic, "We were going out last night, and it was just getting dark. We looked up and saw hundreds of bats coming out of our chimney!" she exclaimed.

Bats in the chimney didn't seem like such a big deal. I called several exterminators, but none of them would handle bats. So, I called a chimney sweep thinking they would know exactly what to do with bats in the chimney. "After that bats are gone, in the night, put a fire in the fireplace. The next morning when the bats return, they'll smell the smoke and won't come back."

Whew, an easy solution. I left this message on her answering machine, and she called back later. "No, no, they're not in the chimney, they're in the attic! Lots of them, thousands. They darken up the sky when they leave. Two have gotten into the house."

I told her I had already called several pest control companies and they didn't know anything about bats. She was a good tenant and had been calling exterminators on her own. In the meantime, she had been doing some calling on her own and found a company that would do the job for around $400.

Our limit on doing repairs with this particular property was $200. We would have to get permission from the owner. I called several other pest companies and could not find any that took care of bats and had no idea where the tenant had found this company to do the extermination. Also, weren't bats considered an endangered species? Was it all of them or just a few types?

Visalia is a small agricultural community in California's Central Valley. I tried calling animal control for information about the bats, but they only dealt with stray dogs and knew nothing about other animals, although someone knew that they were probably fruit bats because a lot of fruit is grown in the area. Animal control suggested I call the local animal shelter. I called and naturally they could tell me nothing about bats.

Since we lived in the San Francisco Bay Area, I decided to call the local animal control there to see what they could tell me about bats. They didn't know anything about bats either, but gave me about five businesses who dealt with bat extraction. Extraction, not extermination.

I called all of them, and one called back. The bat man and I had a very long talk. Bats are indeed endangered species -- all of them. Bats are good for the environment, they help with insect control and their poop makes great fertilizer. In fact, bat poop fertilizer is considered the gourmet of all fertilizers and is very expensive.

Maybe the owner should keep the bats and collect the fertilizer.

Bat man asked me how long the bats had been there and if the units were starting to smell bad. The tenants hadn't complained about the smell. He informed me that male and female bats live apart. Male bats in the attic meant he could come out anytime; but if they were females, he would have to come before the end of May. If the extraction could not be completed before then, he would have to wait until the female bats had their babies weaned and that would delay the extraction until October. That would be a full summer of bat fertilizer accumulating in the attic. If it didn't smell now, it would.

Maybe the owner should forget about fertilizer farming and get those bats out ASAP!

Bat man told me once the extraction was complete the bats would still think the attic was their home, and they would circle around it for hours trying to get back in. The owner needed to be prepared, the bats could end up inside the house.

I told him two had already gotten inside the house, and the tenants had a small child.

He suggested that maybe the tenants should get a rabies shot. As a property manager who owns several rentals, the first thing that came to mind was: lawsuit.

Bat man would come out to Visalia and give a complete estimate for the low cost of $100. Sounded okay. About how much did a complete extraction cost. Depended, but around $1600.

Uh-oh. I knew the owner was a little strapped for cash. He needed to put a new roof on the duplex two years ago and he didn't do it. Note: If a property needs a new roof, get it done right away.

I suggested having a roofer come out and repair the roof at night while the bats were gone. Then they wouldn't be able to get back in the attic. Of course, working on the roof in the dark would create a huge liability for the owner if the roofer were to fall making repairs.

Bat man told me that was a terrible idea. First, not all of the bats leave at night. Several stay home, they're just not that hungry and they want a little space to themselves. The bats that stayed in would die. Had I ever smelt the rotting corpse of a dead bat? No. It was worse than the rotting smell of a dead rat. Having lived a sheltered life, I hadn't smelt that either. "Well, it's the worst smell there is. There's nothing like it. You don't want a bunch of dead bats in your attic. You think your tenants are complaining now."

I told him about the company my tenant had found that would exterminate the bats for $400. Bat man got very upset. Bat exterminations are illegal and they should get their license removed, be fined, go to jail along with the owner and/or whoever hired them -- which meant I wouldn't be hiring them.

I thanked him, and tried to think of other options. What if we just put a big huge bright light on in the attic and left it on 24/7? Maybe the bats would take the hint and leave.

Or, how about this? During the day, the owner puts a new roof on the property. The work on the roof and exposure to the sun would surely encourage the bats to leave. Yes, a whole new roof would cost twice as much, but it would:

    A. give the owner a much needed roof
    B. get rid of the bats
    C. save the cost of bat extraction
    D. all of the above.

If the answer was D, this was the best course of action. But if the answer was only A, and the bats remained, that would be a huge expense creating the additional problem of bats who could not leave at night and a massive mess.

It wasn't my property or my decision. So I had the unpleasant task of calling the owner and telling him the bad news. He usually talked to my partner, and they would discuss things like vacancy and quality of the current tenants and buying more properties. Whenever I spoke to the owner, it had to do with property repair issues. Owners generally don't like it when I come on the phone.

I explained to him about the bats, and told him the approximate cost of the work. A long pause. Maybe we had been disconnected. "Hello?"

"I'm recuperating from the heart attack you just gave me."

And I hadn't even got to the part about the rabies shots and potential owner liability.

I had successfully answered all of the owner's questions about his options. I didn't mention the exterminators because that was the illegal option, but explained why repairing the roof for $200 would seal in many live bats and create a terrible stink. "Pay someone to come out and clean it up," he suggested.

I didn't think that was his best option. We have a hard enough time finding people to do regular repair jobs. How would we ever find someone willing to clear out a bunch of dead bats? Who would do that? What about the possibility of disease?

The owner was not happy. How had the bats gotten there in the first place? Shouldn't a home inspection had found the bats? No, home inspectors don't do roofs, but the home inspector had noted this duplex needed a new roof. The current owner had opted for a two-year roof certification instead, and a roof allowance of $3000 had been taken off the purchase price. The owner's two years were up and he hadn't used that $3000 off the purchase price to put on a new roof.

Leave it to the owner to do things on the cheap. Somehow, he found the same extermination company to kill bats as the tenant. I was very upset. Bats are an endangered species, they don't hurt people, they eat bugs, and their poop is gourmet fertilizer. The idea of killing all those bats sickened me. I warned the owner that bat exterminations are illegal and he could be fined or go to jail.

The owner came to his senses. He conducted his own research and found another bat extraction company who enlightened him. Once that happened, the owner called my partner. "Call these people and get this done, NOW." And we did.

The bat extraction was taken care of legally and expensively. The owner still needs a new roof.

Trees

The day started out normal. It was the middle of the month, rents were all in, all the units were rented and there were no evictions pending. Not a lot to do. My partner and I went out to lunch and ran some errands, and then the cell phone rang, it went to voice mail.

An attorney – who else -- left a rather cryptic message about a dead tree on another property that we manage. He said, "The property has been cited for the tree and he's going to take it to the judge." We couldn't understand the message. There was a dead tree in the back yard of one of the properties we managed. It had been there for years. No one ever received a citation. We thought it was a prank or something.

Still we puzzled over the call. When we got back to the office, we first determined if the person who called was actually an attorney. He was. Okay, but why would an attorney leave such a perplexing message? It sounded like the attorney had issued a citation. Doesn't the city usually issue a citation and post it on the door, give you thirty days to fix the problem and then fine you if you don't? That's how they do it in California. But this was Alabama, and Alabama local laws seemed to be a lot less sophisticated than California.

I called the city and asked if there was a citation for the property with the tree. Two people at the city told me there was an ordinance for tall grass but not for dead trees. One lady I spoke to thought maybe the neighbors were pulling a fast one, but she transferred me over to code enforcement. When the pleasant sounding woman answered, I asked about the tree and if there was a citation on that property.

Suddenly this person started demanding of me who I was, where I was, what's my address, what's my relationship to the property. She didn't sound pleasant anymore, she sounded mean like she was going to attack me. There was indeed a citation on the property.

"But our office never received anything, how could this be?" I asked.

The woman wouldn't answer. She continued to grill me. I was getting a little nervous, like maybe she was going to send the cops out to arrest me. I didn't own the property, I just helped manage it, and the way she was going at me, I didn't even want to admit to that much. I gave her the California office phone number and address.

"Where are you right now," she demanded. I had to admit I was currently in town. "Have you been by the property?" she asked.

"We drove by earlier today," I told her. "I don't understand how you can cite something and not tell anyone about it. Besides I was told you only cited for high grass and weeds."

She informed me that in Alabama they had people who drove by properties specifically to make sure lawns were mowed, and they could cite for whatever they wanted.

"But nobody ever told me. No one ever received a citation."

She didn't care about this, she wouldn't give me the name, but she said there was a warrant out for someone's arrest in relation to the tree. I was shocked. A warrant, what in the world was going on?

When I got off the phone, I was a wreck. So it was my partner's turn to call the city. He spoke to somebody nice who explained the situation to him. Then he talked to the attorney who had left the cryptic message and we were able to piece together what had happened.

Alabama is one of the two nondisclosure states in the country. Nondisclosure basically means let the buyer beware, and boy, should the buy beware. When someone sells a residential property, they don't have to tell you anything about it. They don't have to tell you what's wrong with it or what's good about it.

Nothing. It is up to the buyer to find out any problems for themselves, which can be difficult to do even with home inspections.

When the owners bought the property, the house with the tree had been recently remodeled. It looked really good. We had our home inspector come out and take a look before purchasing and everything was fine. The only problem was the dead tree in the back yard. We were unaware of any ordinance about dead trees, but the former owner knew about it, and didn't disclose that the tree needed to be removed.

The tree was on our list to be taken care of, but not a high priority, because we knew nothing about a citation. Owners generally don't like to spend a lot of money on recently purchased properties where they've already paid out thousands of dollars for a down payment and closing costs.

After spending the afternoon on the phone with the city, with the attorney, back with the city, on top of calling tree removal services for estimates -- we finally heard the entire story.

The city had gotten a complaint from a neighbor and in usual government fashion took their time acting upon it. The former owner received the citation for the tree right before the closing. Since the former owner would no longer own the property, he ignored the citation and didn't tell the new owner or us about it. The tree was not removed, so the former owner received a summons since the property had been in his name at the time. He simply called the city to tell them he no longer owned the property. The city clerk told him that he would still have to come to court and show proof he no longer owned the property. At which point he became belligerent with the clerk, so she remembered him and the tree.

The former owner never showed up to court and the judge issued a warrant for his arrest. When the owner realized he could go to jail, he called the attorney he used for all his closings, and the attorney left the puzzling message with us that didn't make sense.

While my partner and I were trying to figure out what was going on, I called the city and happened to speak to the same clerk who the former owner had been confrontational with; and guess what, she remembered the tree, she remembered him, and she was a bitch with me.

The issue was finally ironed out. The city sent a citation to the new owner. By the time he received it, we already had the tree removed.

The Sexual Predator

Megan's Law is a Federal law requiring states to maintain public registries of convicted sex offenders and of persons who have committed crimes against children. Individual states decide how this information is to be disseminated. California has a particularly good web site for the public to learn where registered sex offenders live. One evening my partner and I were looking at the web site and searching all the addresses of the properties we managed just to see if any sex offenders lived nearby.

We owned a duplex in Corning, and typed in that address. To my surprise, it indicated a sex offender currently lived in one of the units. How could that be? According to the photograph, he was a middle-aged white male.

When we purchased the property, both units had been empty, as in vacant, as in no one was living there. We had both units rented out to older single women who were on SSI. From the date of our purchase, no man ever lived on the property.

A woman named Fran lived in the unit where the website indicated the male sexual predator resided. Fran could barely walk and relied heavily upon a wheelchair. When we rented to Fran, we could tell she was a woman who enjoyed learning and trying new things. She was a quite large for the small place, but one woman, living alone barely able to walk would want a small place.

We emailed the Megan's Law website agency indicating this man had not lived at the property for over three years and to please update their records.

Several months later, after acquiring some new properties, we went to Megan's Law website again to see what type of people were living in these neighborhoods. We also went back to the address in Corning to see if it had been properly updated. The site still indicated a sexual offender lived in the unit. We emailed again, knowing it was an exercise in futility.

A few weeks later, we received a strange phone call from my new my tenant in the duplex in Corning telling me she was engaged to be married, and they would be moving to a larger place.

How does a housebound woman in a wheelchair meet someone to get engaged? Oh well, not our business.

The next month when collecting the rent, we met her fiancé. He was an older man about the same age as the tenant and seemed very nice. We spoke a little while, and she asked if I had anyplace larger where they could rent. Not at the time, but I did have a three bedroom coming up in a few months, it was very nice. The rent was more than they could afford.

On Saturdays we often drove from the Bay Area to Visalia to take care of issues with the properties we managed in Southern California. My partner would drive the three hours down, we would deal with the rentals, and then my job was to drive back. We left early in the morning, and I was closing my eyes half asleep while my partner drove. I bolted upright. "That man, that man who's engaged to Fran, he's the same man in that picture for Megan's law. I'm sure of it!"

I called my other tenant in the duplex; and asked her to look online and verify that picture of the sex offender was actually Fran's fiancé.

The tenant immediately called back in a panic. "Yes that's him, and if you don't get him out of there I'm moving. My granddaughter comes to visit and I'm not putting her in harms way."

"He doesn't live there." How naïve I was, still am sometimes.

"Oh, yes he does. He never leaves."

So I called Fran. She assured me everything was fine, he wasn't living there and they would soon be finding a bigger place. But she wasn't sounding like the Fran we had rented to, she sounded out of it, very tired, very weak, and a bit whiny. However, Fran wasn't a well woman.

There was nothing we could do at the moment, as long as they would move as promised. But then Fran's rent check bounced. Now it was easy. Give Fran and her fiancé a Pay or Quit and get them out.

After receiving the notice, Fran called. "Please, please, put the check in again, it will clear," she begged.

The check still didn't clear. I informed her about the bounced check fees and late fees. Every time I called, she would heave this big, heavy sigh like it was such a burden to pick up the phone.

I told her she had to get that guy out of there. "Why?" she whined, "He's helping me."

I explained to her who he was, and that I had concerns about her safety. He needed to be out. She heaved another big sigh, got off the phone and called me back a few minutes. "I was married to him before," she said. "He's trying very hard to reform, we'll make good on the rent..." and the whining continued.

She sent us another check, which also bounced. In the meantime, we found out that the convicted sex offender with whom she now lived, had molested her own daughter -- and Fran still wanted him back.

We went to the police and told them about the sex offender living at our house and how he wasn't supposed to be there. They checked Megan's law website, and when his picture popped up at that address said he was indeed supposed to be there.

We explained he hadn't lived there for three years and now he was back and we didn't want him there. The police could have cared less. What are we paying these guys for? To give us speeding tickets?

We also attempted to call his parole officer and tell her what was going on. The parole officer never called back.

We had no choice but to continue with the eviction based on non-payment of rent. After we filed and served the Unlawful Detainer Action, someone intervened on the tenant's behalf.

A man from a social service agency called asking me to please stop the eviction. He promised that the guy be removed from the property and would be gone by the end of the month.

Fran had recently qualified for Section 8 housing and also would be getting a payee to manage her income.

Apparently this guy had been taking her SSI money and spending it on stuff he wanted, thus the bounced rent checks. If we were patient, we would be paid in full for the lost rent, the bounced check fees and the late fees. Our mortgage company should be so patient.

Vacancies cost money. We took the deal. In a few months, Fran was paid up on rent, court costs, late and bounced check fees. Better yet, the guy was gone. She stayed and paid her rent on time for another seven years. What more can a landlord ask?

By the way, although the man has been out of the unit for years, he still remains on the Megan's Law website as still living at that address.

Mental Illness

We had a vacancy we were showing at least once a day sometimes twice. Finally a young woman, Cicily put in an application and she seemed like she would make a really great tenant. Before she could move in, we agreed to do some hauling, cleaning and paint the interior.

She wanted the house bad enough that she was willing to pay her deposit to hold the property while we completed the work. When all the junk was hauled away, Cicily wanted to look at the place again. She heard we had another house for rent nearby and wanted to take a look at it before committing to the one she had seen. Fine.

Cicily parked her SUV in the driveway. We never park in the driveway for safety reasons, and because there was no room for off-street parking on the busy street in front of the house, we parked on a near-by side street. You could see our car from the house. Cicily was inside her SUV, and we were making arrangements for her to follow us to the other rental. My partner went to our parked car, but I had forgot to lock one of the doors in the house and Cicily wanted to look the place over one more time.

As we came outside and walked toward Cicily's car, a woman stopped her car in the middle of street staring at us. The FOR RENT sign was still out and I simply figured she wanted to know how much we were asking for rent. She asked me something unintelligible, and cars were starting to back up behind hers. I just said, "I don't know."

This answer incensed her and she got out of the car, oblivious of traffic and started coming over to the house. In the meantime, the cars piling up behind her started honking. The woman had the sense to get back in her car and turn the corner on the side street where we were parked. She simply stopped her car in the middle of the street and got out and stormed over.

"You're dealing drugs here," she accused.

Huh? I was so stunned I didn't know what to say.

The tenant said, "No, no, she's the owner and I'm renting the house."

"No you're not, you're dealing drugs here." The neighbor next door was out watering his lawn. "Call the police," she ordered the guy. "They're doing drugs."

The tenant and I just looked at each other. We decided just to leave and let the crazy woman rant. I went back to my car only to see that the crazy woman was still in the tenant's face. The next thing I knew, Cicily pushed the crazy woman to the ground. Cicily then got inside her car.

The crazy woman stood back up, went and lay underneath the rear wheels of Cicily's vehicle. Cicily didn't realize the woman was there. When she started backing up her SUV, the woman stood with her back against the vehicle as if to keep it from moving. Cicily slowly backed out, still unaware the crazy woman was behind her car. It was kind of funny to watch the woman being pushed out of the driveway by the car. When Cicily realized the woman was there, she stopped and hurried out of her car.

We called 911 several times, Cicily called 911 four times and the next door neighbor also called a couple of times. It took the local police over thirty minutes to show up.

The crazy woman managed to get it together when the police arrived, and even though we told the cop the woman was nuts, he didn't understand. He actually seemed to be taking her side! Fortunately another policeman arrived who happened to know Cicily, and after talking to her understood the situation and made the crazy woman go away.

The first cop who still couldn't grasp the whole story told the policeman who arrived later, "That woman didn't seem quite right."

I hate to imagine what would have happened if Cicily's friend hadn't been on the scene and the crazy woman actually convinced the cop we were drug dealers. Yikes! The cop may have been one of the city's finest, but definitely not one of their brightest.

Chapter Seventeen
Managing Long Distance

Many real estate gurus tell you to purchase property no further than twenty minutes away from your home. The idea is to reduce travel time and make managing your rentals easier. Good advice, in theory.

In reality, finding properties that work within your budget and financial goals may be located much further than a twenty-minute drive. The property that meets your financial capabilities may be in another town or even in another state hundreds of miles away.

In spite of the distance, you still may be able to manage the rental yourself without the aid of a property manager. Our small property management firm handled rentals from in California from Redding to Visalia, and at the same time managed properties in Alabama. Albeit challenging, we can attest to the fact it is possible to effectively manage properties long distance. With the advent of computers, scanners, printers and cell phones it's easier than you might think. Here's how.

Travel

You have to be able to visit your property as necessary, usually when it is vacant. The good news is that all of your trips to the property will be tax deductable. Emergency situations may require that you take time off work to visit the property. Otherwise, you may have to schedule vacation time and days off to take care of rental issues. If you have property that is out of state or requires a plane ride and/or overnight stay, it becomes important to make every trip to the property count.

Start advertising your vacancy a week before you plan to be at the property, so when you arrive you can show the rental to as many people as possible. Hopefully, you will have enough interest that you receive one or two good applications the same day. If you don't, put up some signage in the neighborhood as discussed in Chapter 2.

If you are unable to rent the property while you are in town and you don't have friends or family in the area who can assist you, enlist the broker who helped you purchase the home to show it. Paying the broker may be cheaper than repeated trips to the area. To help defray costs for yourself or the person showing the property, charge a reasonable application fee, and whoever shows the property can keep the money. We enlist neighbors or other tenants and tell them to collect a $10 application fee, which can add up if several people are interested in the property.

Any person other than yourself – unless they are your licensed property management firm – will not be able to negotiate terms or prices about the property. Neither can they select the tenant on your behalf. Their job is to show the property and convey to you their thoughts and opinions about the applicants. They may be able to answer basic questions, but you can always speak to the applicant over the phone and address their concerns.

Whoever is showing the home can fax the application to you along with the applicant's pay-check stubs. When you get the place rented, you can pay your non-employee a $100 finder's fee. Using the internet, you can research the validity of the application. In cases where you are unable to meet the tenant, you may want to perform a credit and background check only on those applicants who you are seriously considering.

At some point, you should come out and meet your new tenants, sign the lease and give them keys. However, as long as the person who showed the property is not negotiating, that person can be your liaison for the signing of the lease and giving the new tenants keys. Note: You as the landlord must sign the lease and not the person who is helping you.

In your lease, have the tenants go to the bank to pay their rent. Make sure you lease has a posting fee in case the tenants are late payers. The posting fee should be large enough to pay for the cost of a process server. On the lease, possibly in large, bold letters, have contact information where you can be reached regarding repairs and emergencies. Include phone number and email so documents can be attached. If you use a voice-over Internet service like Skype®, you can purchase a phone number with a local area code for your tenants to call you.

Until you are certain you have a good tenant who isn't going to bring a bunch of riff-raff into the house, you will need to go out occasionally to see how things are going. Once you have a good tenant, you can limit your trips to once or twice a year.

Process Server/Attorney

A good process server can post all your notices and start the eviction procedures. If you are having difficulties locating a process server, call private investigators as they will often perform that service also. Find someone who will send you an invoice or take credit cards. The process server also needs to keep you informed of what they are doing and if they are unable to get the tenant served.

Being out of town, it will be difficult to file the paperwork for any evictions. However, as more and more courts are trudging into the twenty-first century, many of the necessary forms are online. You can fill them out and mail it with your check or have a process server submit them for you.

Of course, you can always have an attorney handle the eviction from start to finish. Before attempting to manage long distance, it is a good idea to have selected an eviction service or attorney you can use if the need arises. You also should find out if you will need to be present for any court proceedings or if the attorney can be in court without you.

Repairs

A tenant in need of repairs is as simple as having a local phone book. These are usually available to be picked up at the chamber of commerce. Handymen often advertise in the local newspapers. While in town, you should meet some handymen and give them a small job or two to test their reliability. As telephone books and newspapers become obsolete, you will have to rely on the internet to find your service providers.

The most common repairs are plumbing and heating/air. A repair person is a phone call away, and will usually go out and give free estimates. And yes, the service provider will often try to take advantage of you because you are out of town, but you're not falling for it. Call at least two service providers and compare estimates. Whenever a service provider wants to install a new unit such as a heating or air conditioning system, call someone else. Larger firms will usually take credit cards over the phone, however you must insist on receiving a copy of the invoice before payment in order to reflect the expense on your taxes.

Rather than letting your tenants know you live out of town, it is better to let them think you are simply busy and unavailable. Having a local number on your cell phone or computer helps give the illusion of proximity, as well as setting up a local address by renting a private mail box. You can pick up your mail while in town inspecting your properties or pay a fee and have your mail forwarded. These measures are not absolutely necessary, but may help your tenants feel more secure knowing you are around.

Long distance property management has its drawbacks. A good tenant will live at the property for many years and take good care of it. Once your rental is stabilized, you can go out occasionally to check on the exterior and make arrangements to see the interior. If the rental needs paint, roof or other repairs you can get estimates and have the work completed while you are around.

Vacation

Every once in awhile you should take a real vacation – not the trip to the property vacation – but a real vacation. Plan your trip toward the middle of the month after all the rents are in. When you are going to be out of cell phone range such as camping, cruising or in another country, make sure the tenant has someone else to call in case of an emergency. Give your tenants a list of favorite handymen and repair people who you trust, so the tenant can call if something goes wrong. Also call your repair people and tell them you are leaving and what you will and won't pay for.

We had a triplex where each unit was rented to fragile older women. They paid the rent on time, but couldn't lift a finger to help themselves. Constantly there were minor problems: a running toilet, evaporative cooler filters needing changed, a leaky pipe, etc. We had a reliable handyman we always called for these repairs. It got to the point where the tenants would just call him and he would come out do the repair and bill us later. He knew his repair limit was anything under $100. Make sure your handyman knows your limit.

It seems like tenants have a sixth sense when it comes to landlords leaving. Inevitably the week before leaving there more than usual repair issues. In some ways, that is good. You can leave knowing the repairs have been made and everything is fine.

Out of Town Feasibility Check

Here are some questions to ask yourself before managing your properties from a long distance:

- Do I have any friends who can help me show the property and who can drive by the property on a regular basis?

- Will enlisting a friend to help have a negative impact on our relationship?

- Is anyone else who I trust such as a real estate broker available to show vacant rentals?

- Do I have a least two handymen who can make repairs on the property?

- How much does a process server charge for same day service?

- Have I lined up an eviction attorney or eviction service?

- If the tenant answers an eviction complaint will I have to be present for the court day or can an attorney represent me?

Make note of any other concerns you may have and address your issues. If managing long distance is going to be too much trouble, the next chapter explains how to find a good property manager.

Chapter Eighteen

Property Management

Many owners of rental property tend to think all a property manager does is sit back and collect rents, and therefore doesn't have much value. After reading this book, you have a pretty good idea what property management is really like. Go back to Chapter 1 and ask yourself if you have what it takes: the time, the energy, the stamina, the patience, and the fortitude. Dealing with tenants will harden you and shift your thinking of others toward the jaded and cynical side. You may come to a point where you stop believing anything anybody says.

If you decide you don't have what it takes or you're tired of messing with rental properties and want to hand everything over to a property management company, you need to realize that no property management firm is going to care about your property like you do.

Just like anything else, property managers will promise you everything and deliver very little. If you ask them for addresses of other properties they manage so you can drive by and take a look at how well they are being maintained, the firm will give you the addresses of nice looking properties in higher end areas and fail to mention the crap that they also manage.

Marketing

One of the disadvantages about property managers is that they often do not aggressively market the property. Whenever they advertise in the paper and other media, they will pass that cost on to you. They will put their For Rent signs on the property, but often they don't put the sign in highly visible places.

Many property management firms like to tack on a sign on the building itself: Managed By Me, Myself and I Property Management Firm, with their phone number underneath. When a prospective tenant calls, they will hear a recorded message detailing all the available properties for rent and instructing them on how to get an application. In other words, your property may become lost in the firms long list of vacancies. Many property management firms have properties that stay needlessly vacant for a long time.

Whenever we call a property management firm to compare their services and charges with ours, and they think they are speaking to a prospective tenant, they have been curt and rude. Only when they realize we are calling about hiring them as a management firm of our own properties do they become very solicitous.

Some property management companies are notorious for failing to do repairs. They do this because they know the owner doesn't want to hear about yet another costly repair. This creates disgruntled tenants who start to threaten not to pay rent and start destroying the property. On the other hand, we have been fired by owners for making necessary repairs, so we understand the balancing act of keeping a client versus a happy tenant.

If your property happens to be in a rough neighborhood, it may be difficult to find a property manager. It seems most of them prefer to handle rentals in areas where it is easy to find a good tenant. Who wouldn't?

Cost

One of the first things you need to find out is what the property management firm is going to charge you. Some firms take a flat percentage of the rent, often ten percent, but other firms will also take the first month's rent plus a percentage. Your decision to hire a property management firm should not be based exclusively on price, there are other issues to consider.

If you do the math, the real money in property management comes from application fees, late fees charged to the tenant, service repair fees charged to you, and renting fees charged to you. Therefore, a property management firm stands to make more money when the properties are not stable and there is a constant flux of people moving in and out. Not to say a property management firm would do that, but it is something to keep in mind.

Repairs

You won't know if a property management firm doesn't do repairs for the tenant, but you can definitely find out if the company adds a surcharge for you to pay for handling the repair. Ask if they have a handyman on staff and what companies they call for service. Make sure you receive a copy of the invoice of all repairs. Feel free to call the phone number on the invoice to ensure the repair was performed at your property's address.

Evictions

Most property managers will post the Pay or Quit notice, and then hand the issue over to an attorney. This is expensive. See if you can find a property management firm who will also act as an eviction service and do the paperwork through the serving of the unlawful detainer action. Find out who the firm uses for evictions and how much the attorney will charge.

Move-Outs

When someone moves out, the rental usually needs some work. It possibly just needs a thorough cleaning or it may need paint, new carpet and other fix-up. Most property management firms will tell the owner they need to get it rent ready and you must either do it yourself or find someone to do it. Sometimes the firm will give you some people to call, and often will they help coordinate the effort. Some firms will make the rental completely rent ready and charge you for the service. Finding a manager who will also help you with maintenance with the property is invaluable.

Unfortunately many property management firms will determine that the property needs to be in pristine condition before putting it on the rental market. The agent will insist that you make it rent-ready to their specifications.

A pristine rental shows better and is easier to rent, but does not guarantee a better quality tenant. It is distressing to spend a lot of money making a place "showable" only to have it trashed by tenants in less than three months. In theory, when the tenant comes into a property that is fixed-up and looking good, it should also have less repair issues. However, in high turnover areas, making a property "rent-ready" every time a tenant leaves can become very costly. What's more, property management firms tend to send the damages caused by the tenant to collections, and any repayments that come in goes to the firm and not to you.

Conclusion

One of the disadvantages of hiring a property management firm is you lose control of the rental process. Although a property management firm may cost you more money in the long run, perhaps the peace of mind of not having to deal with tenant issues is a better choice. Ultimately whether to manage your rentals yourself or hire a property management firm is a personal choice.

The idea of this book was not to act as a legal guide, that's what attorneys are for, and you should always consult your attorney on any legal matter. Neither was the purpose of this book to encourage you to manage your own rentals or discourage you. The purpose of the book was to give you an idea of what property management can be like. The other purpose was to give those of you determined to manage your own properties some guidelines to make the job easier and to help you find better quality tenants.

Once you have good paying tenants in you rental, you can lay back, relax, and collect rent...at least for awhile.

ABOUT THE AUTHORS

J. Elaine Taylor, MBA and David Blum, DBA have managed residential income properties for over twelve years. They also wrote the book *Real Life Real Estate Investing: A Practical Guide for the First Time Investor.*